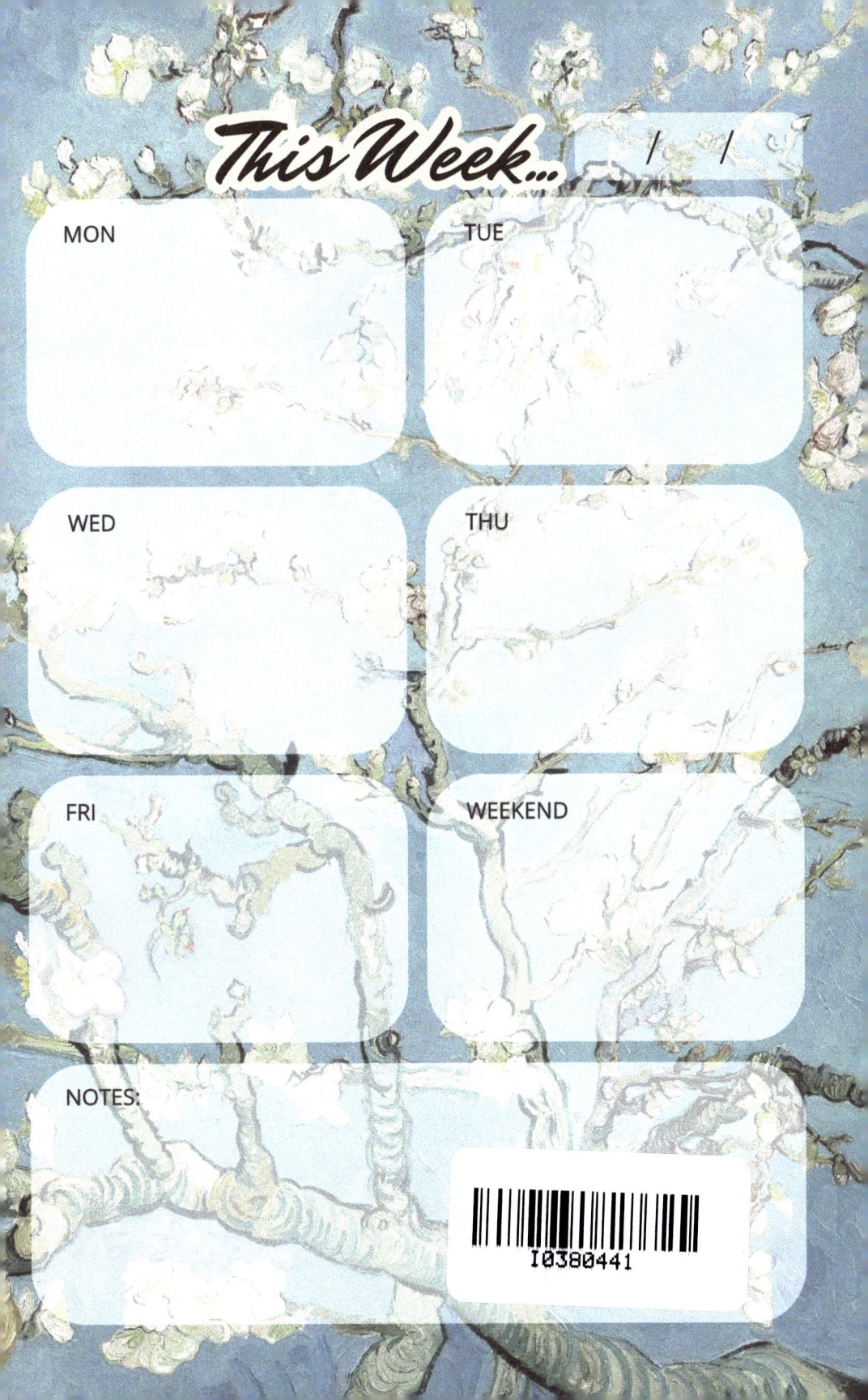

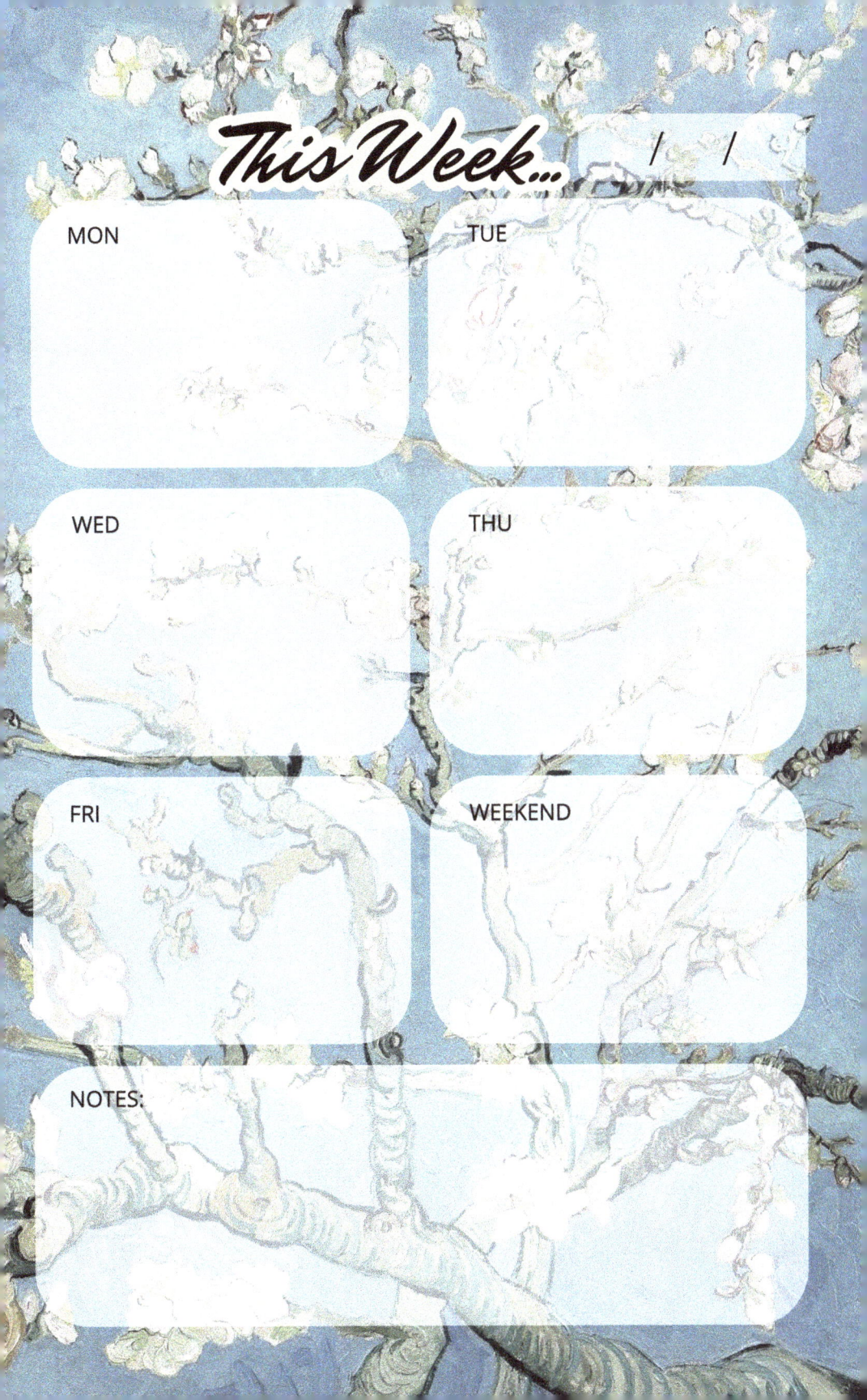

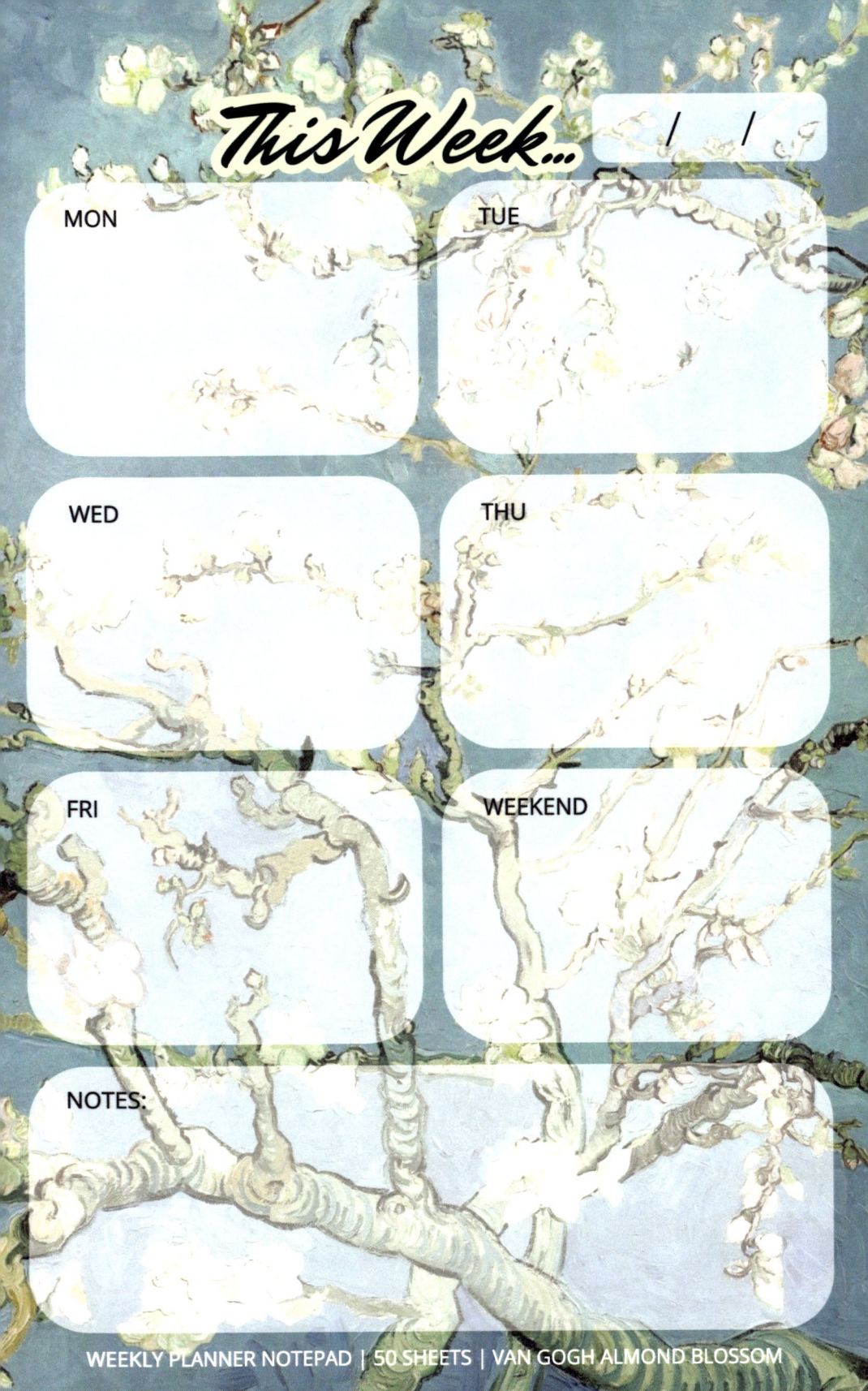

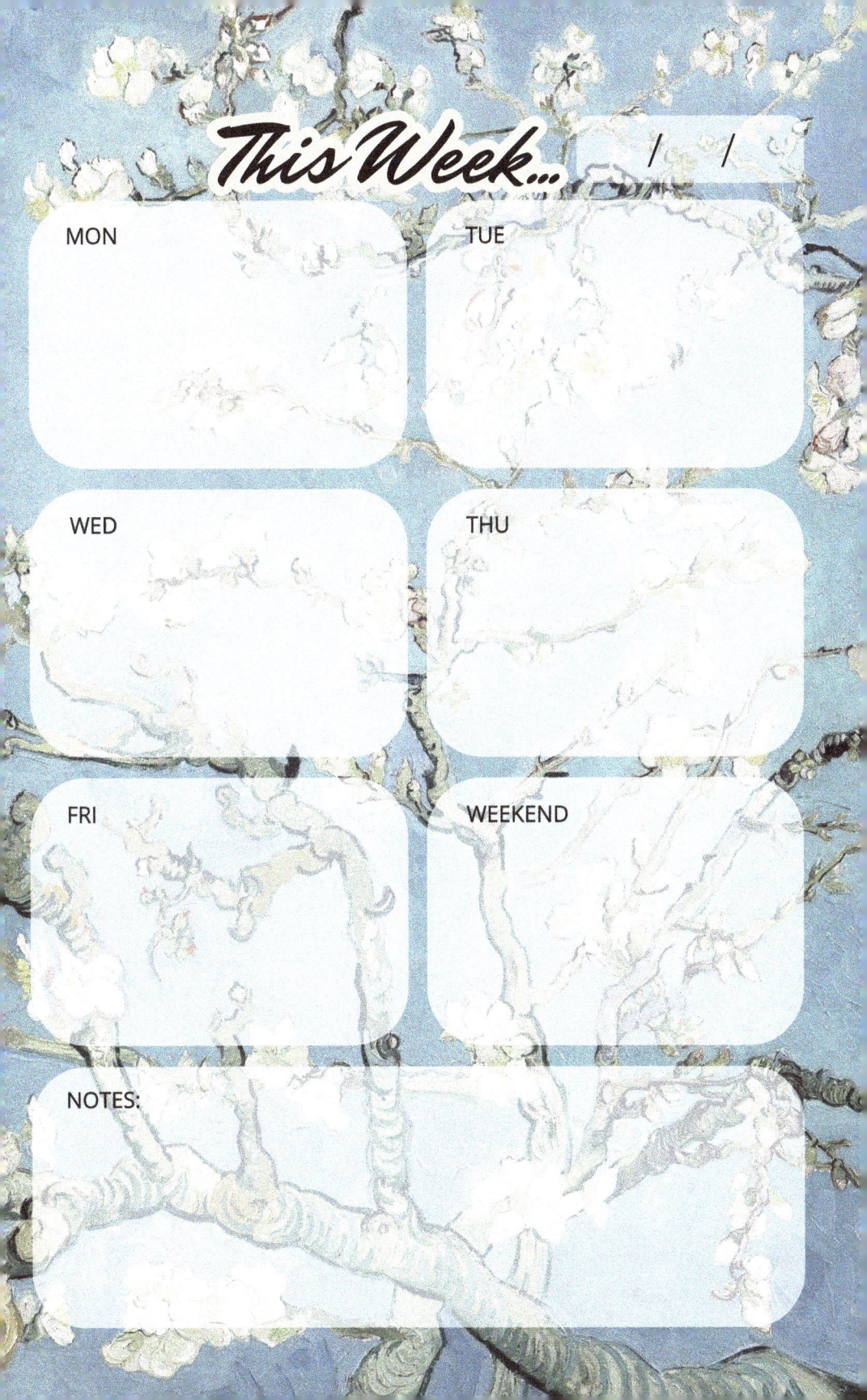

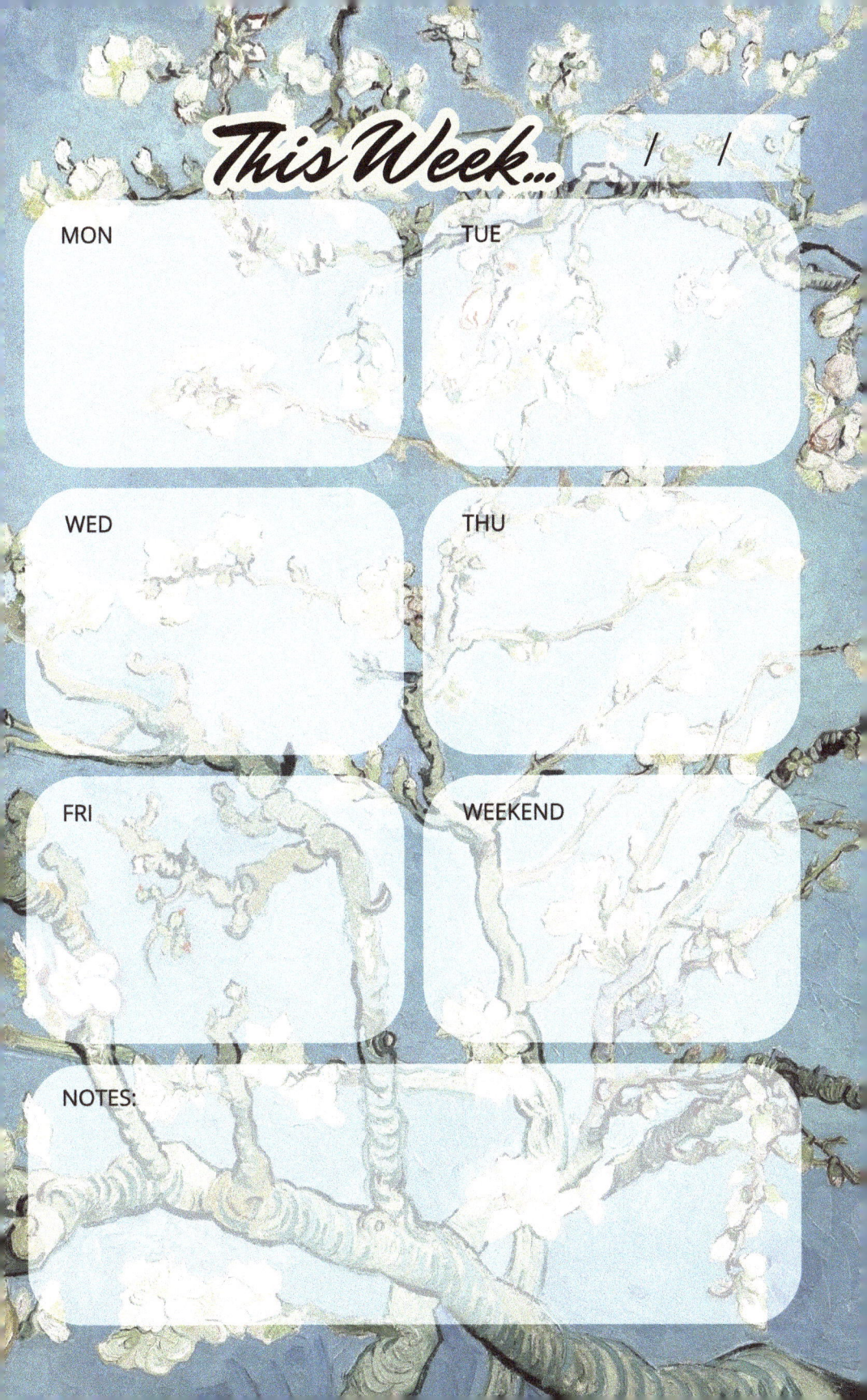

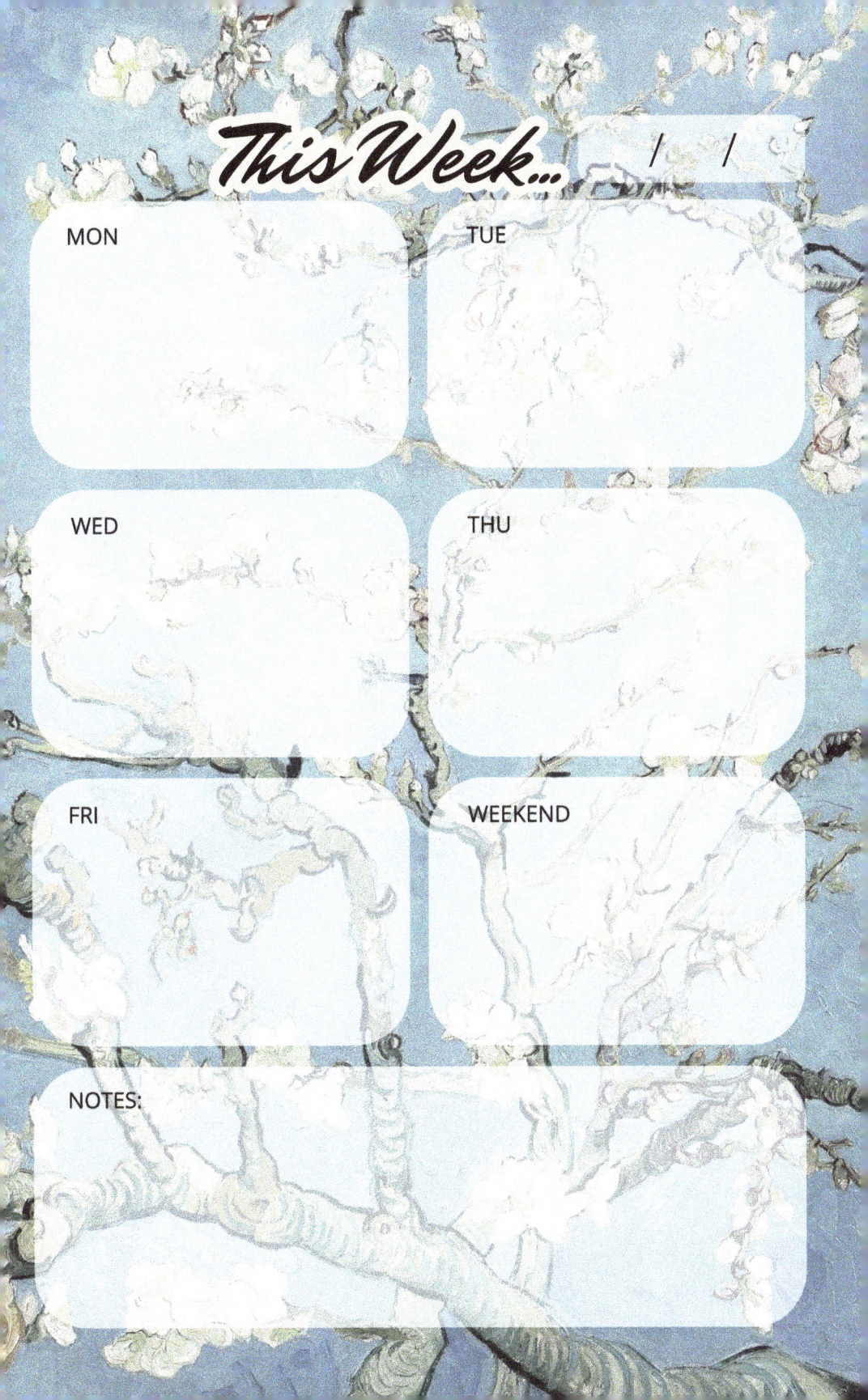

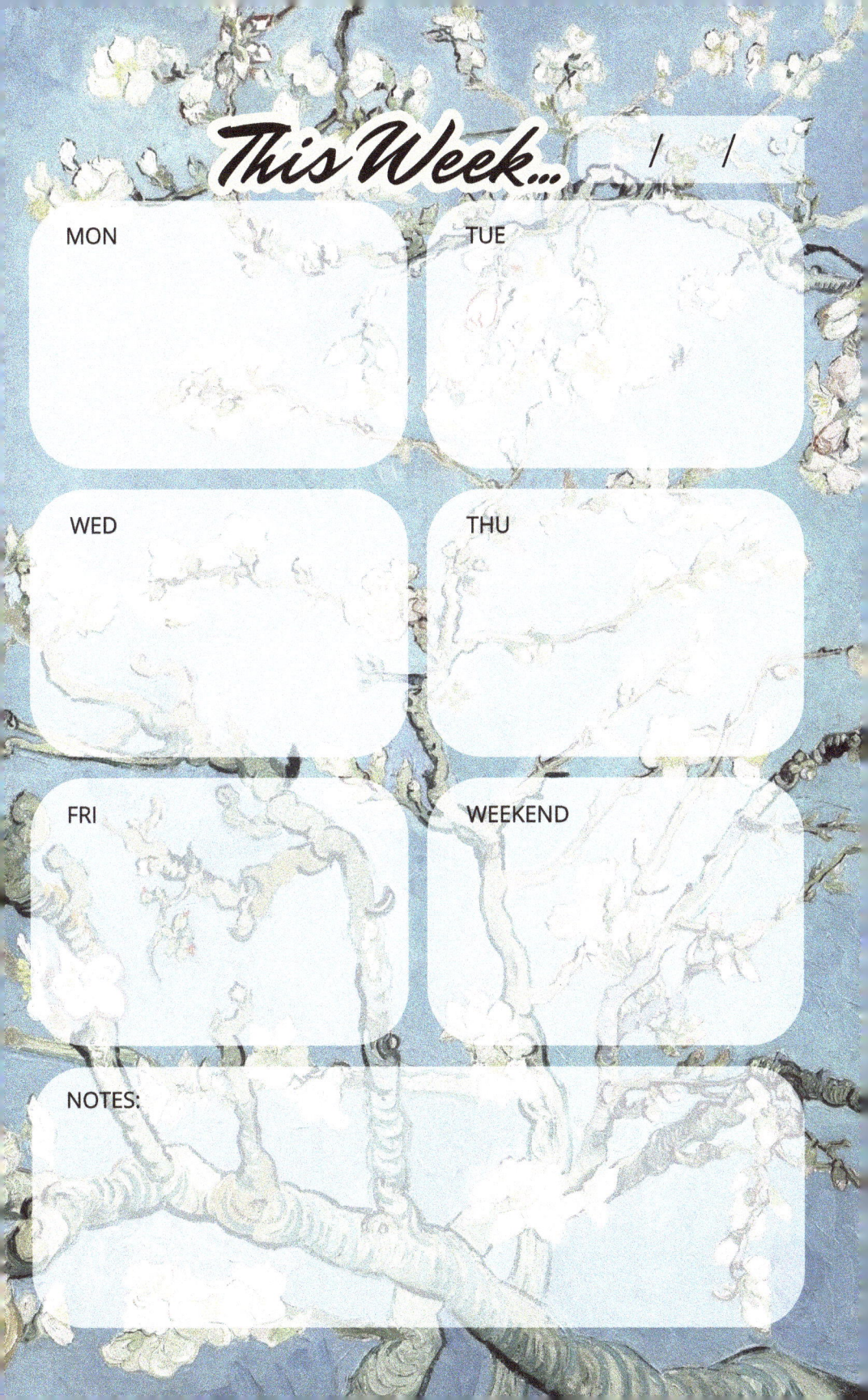

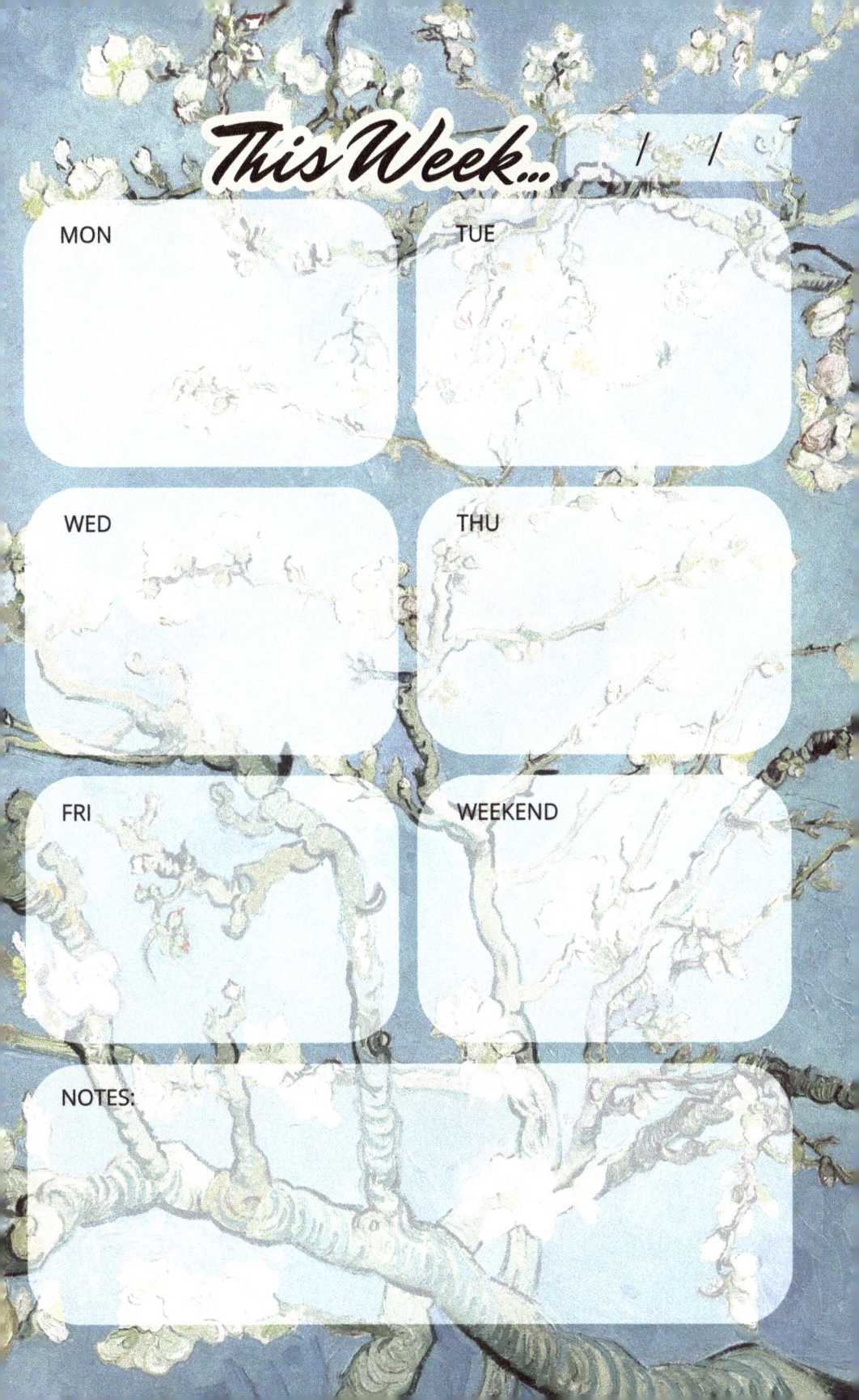

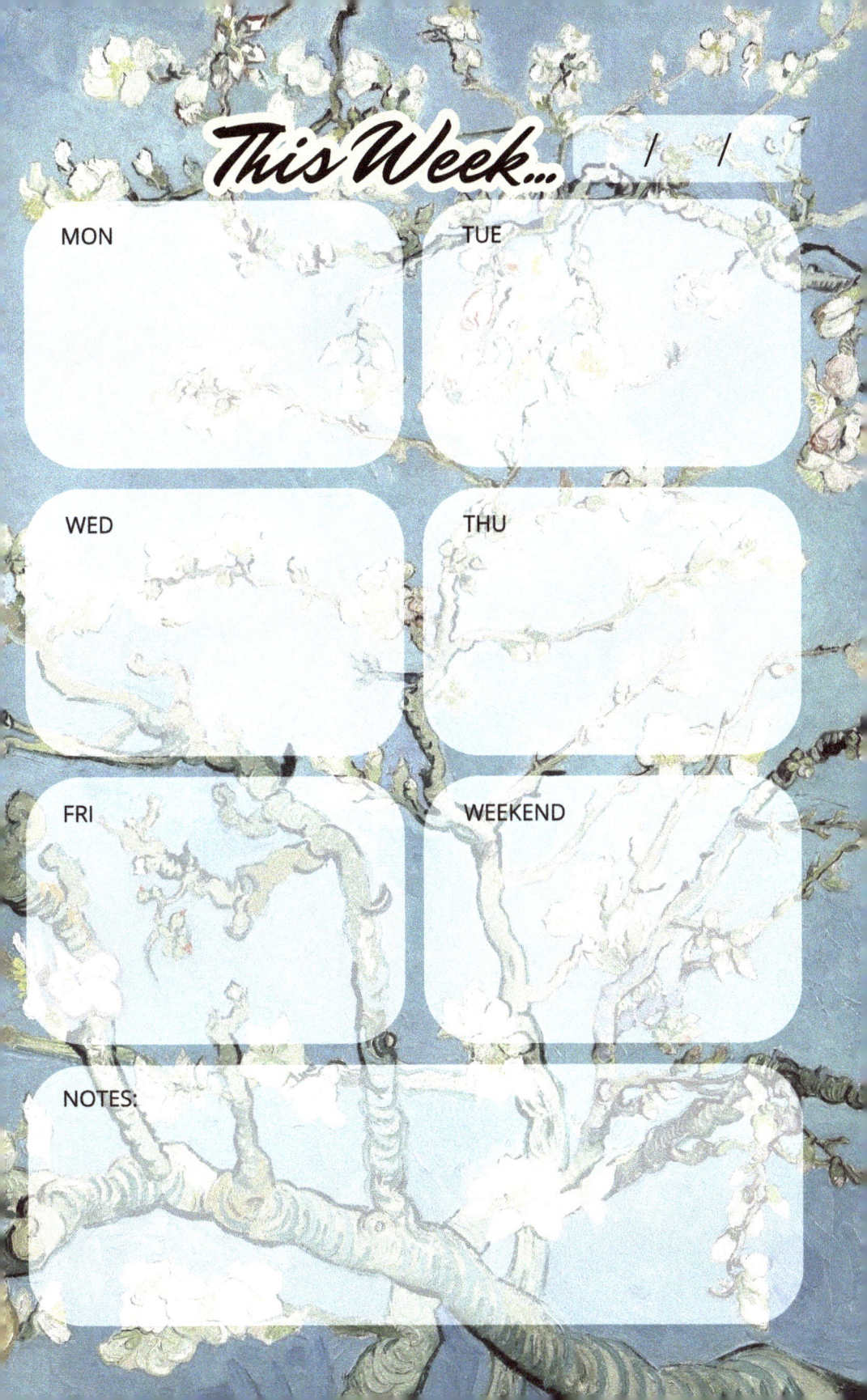

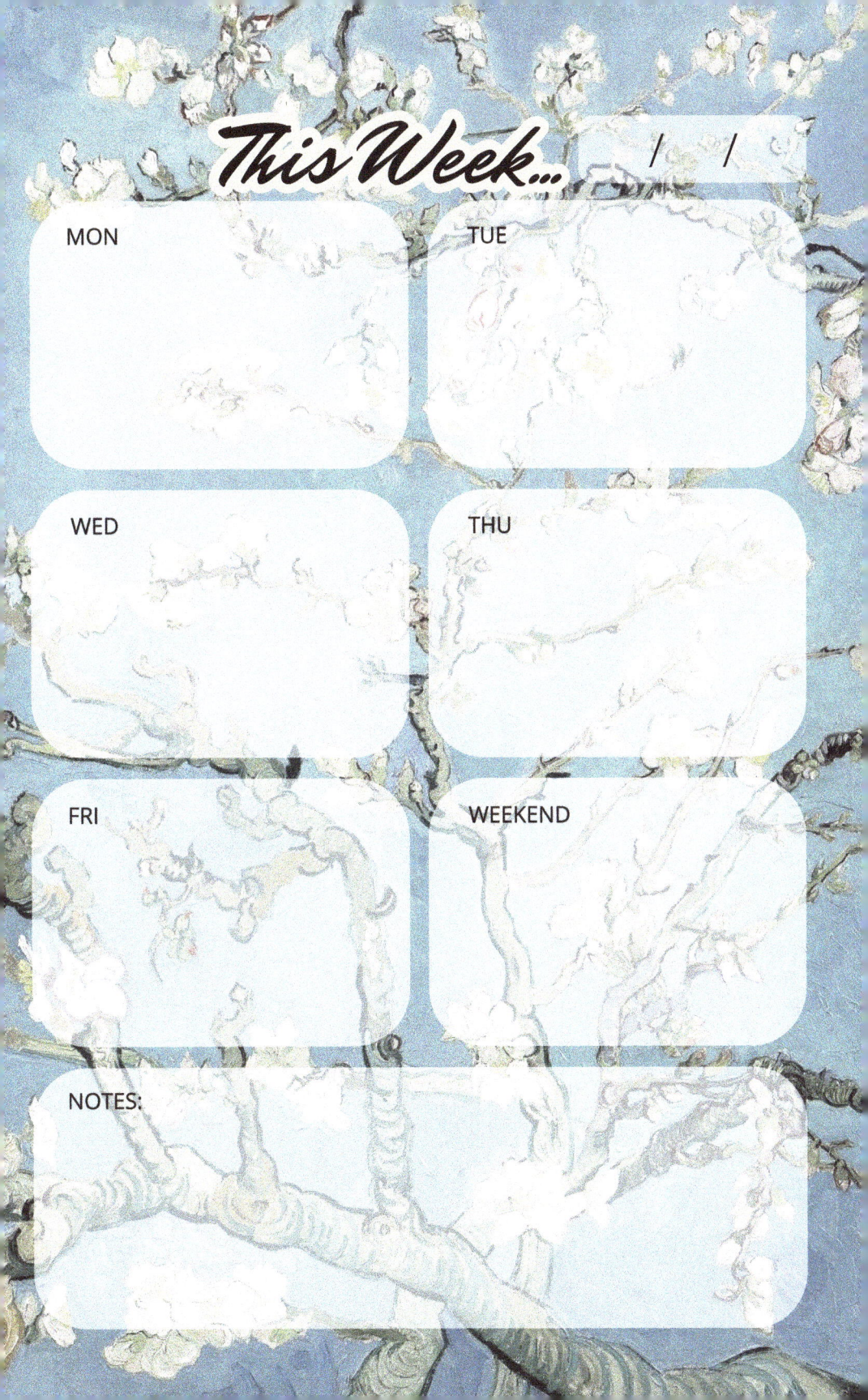

This Week... / /

MON

TUE

WED

THU

FRI

WEEKEND

NOTES:

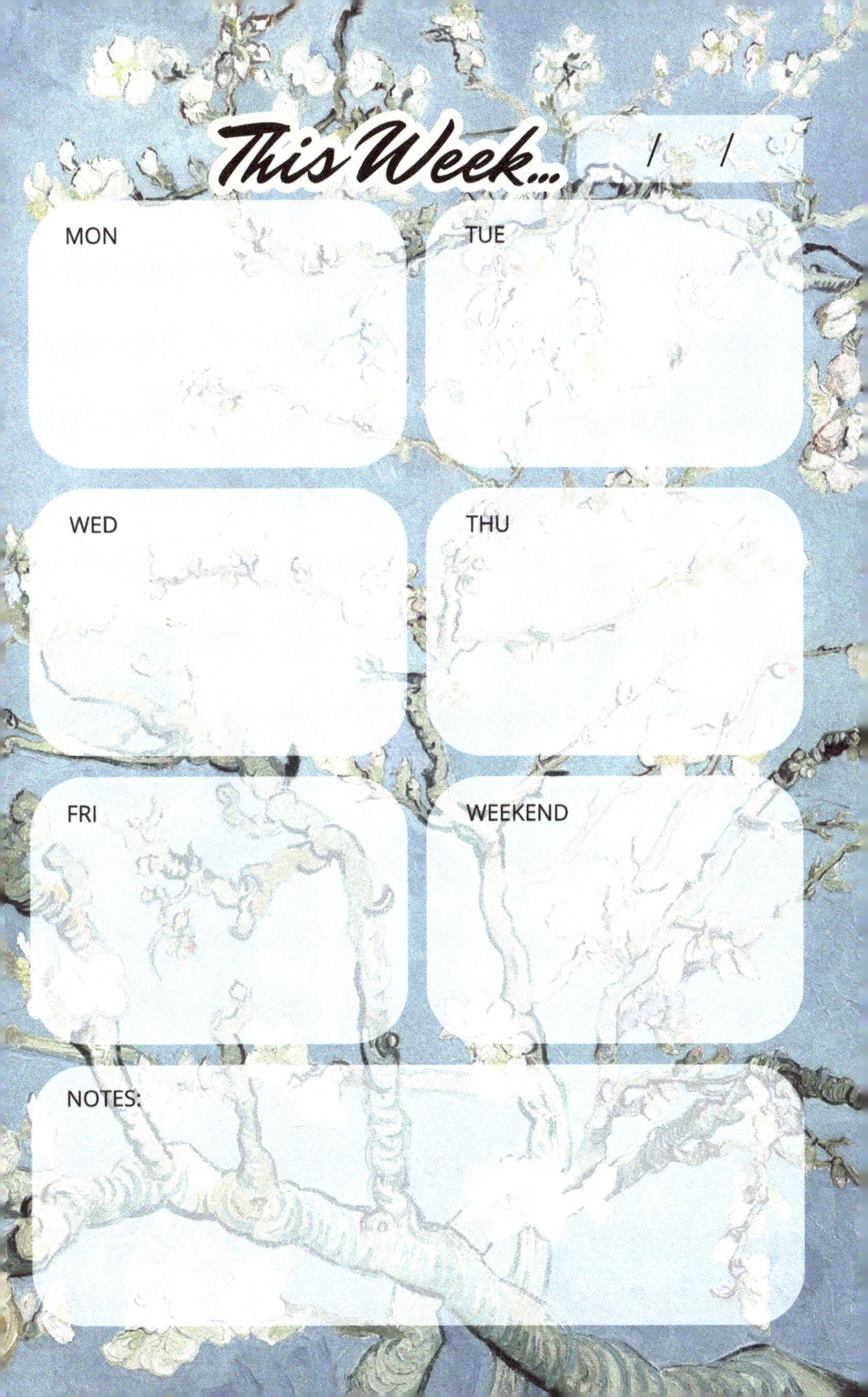

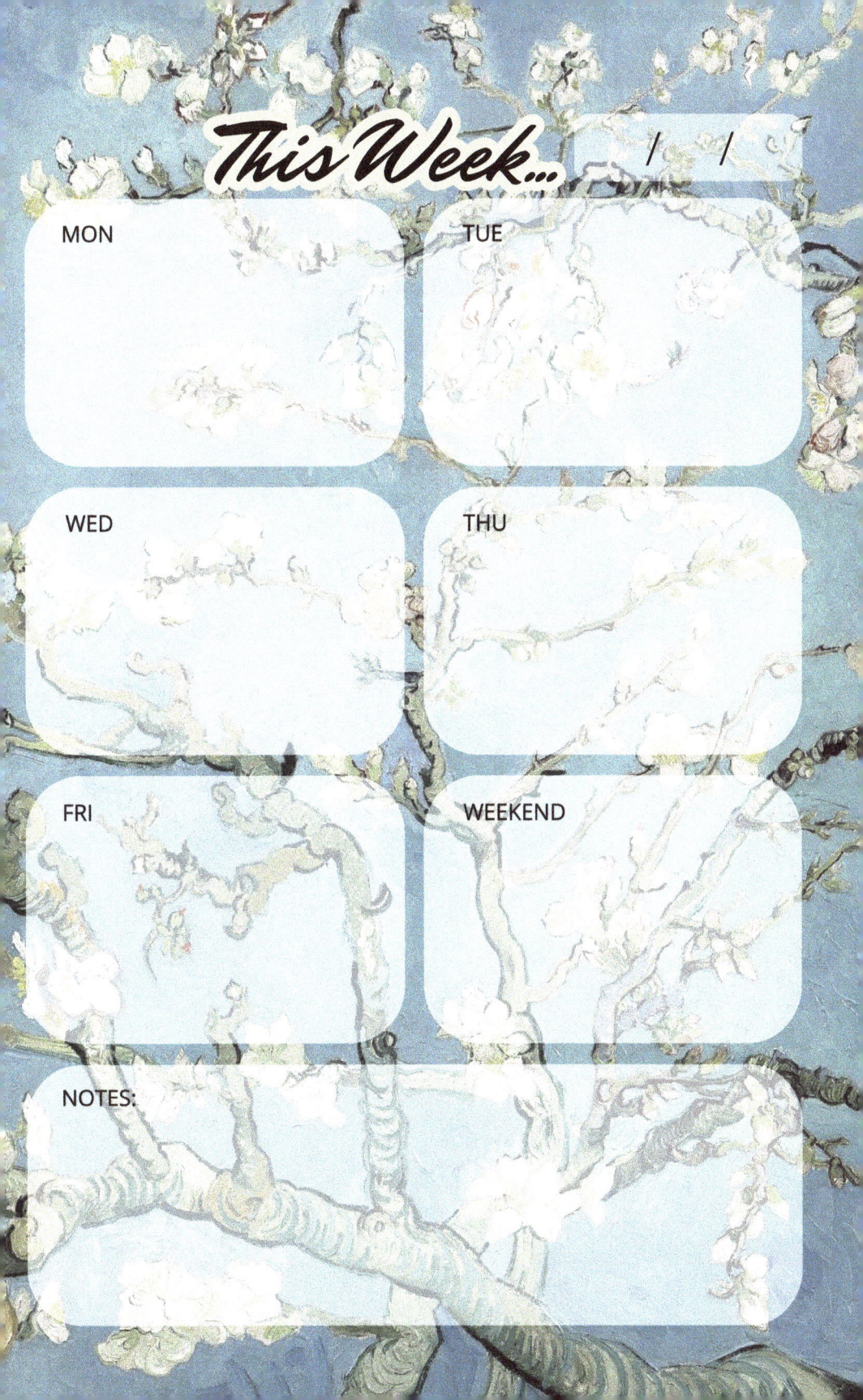

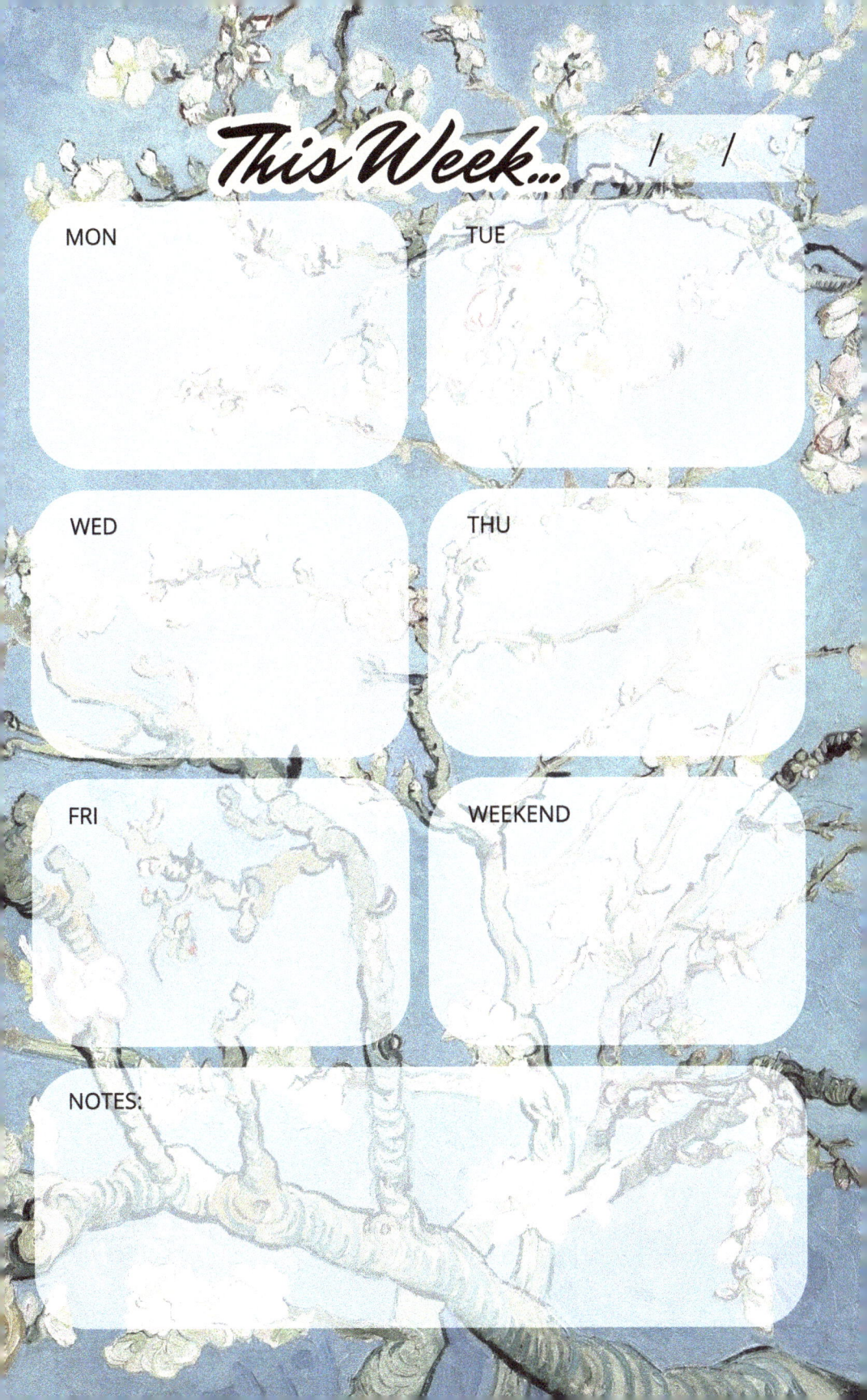

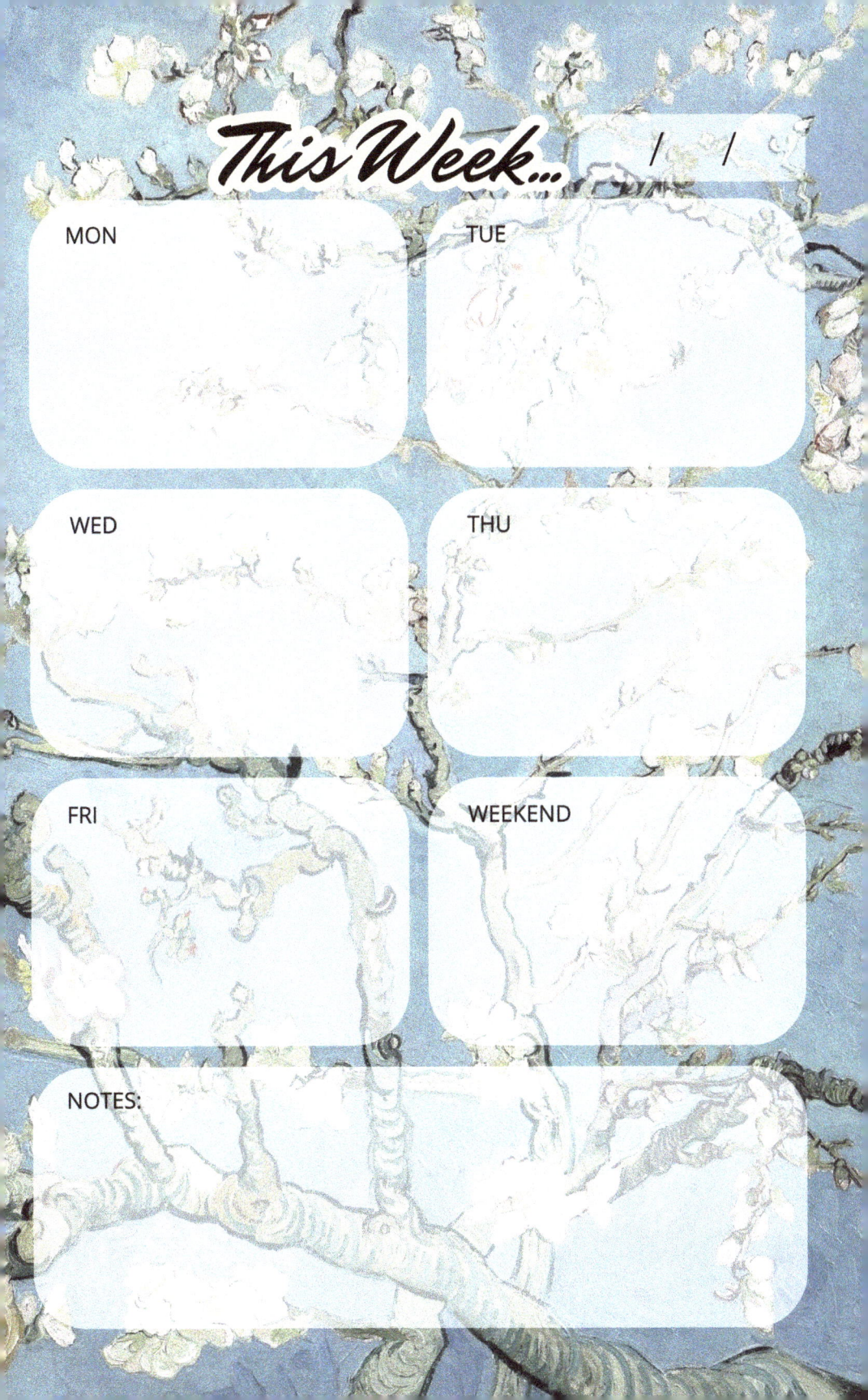

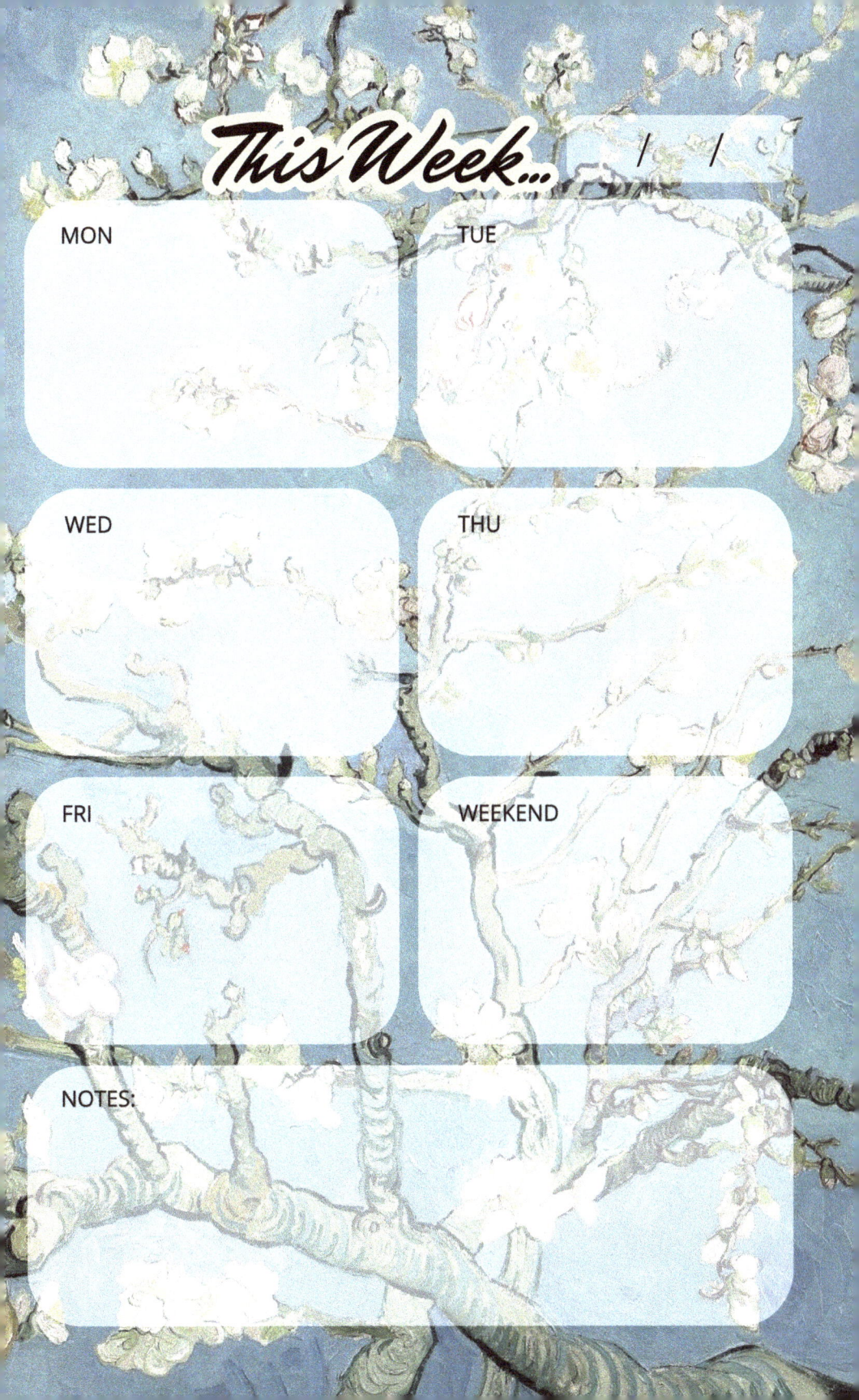

This Week... / /

MON

TUE

WED

THU

FRI

WEEKEND

NOTES:

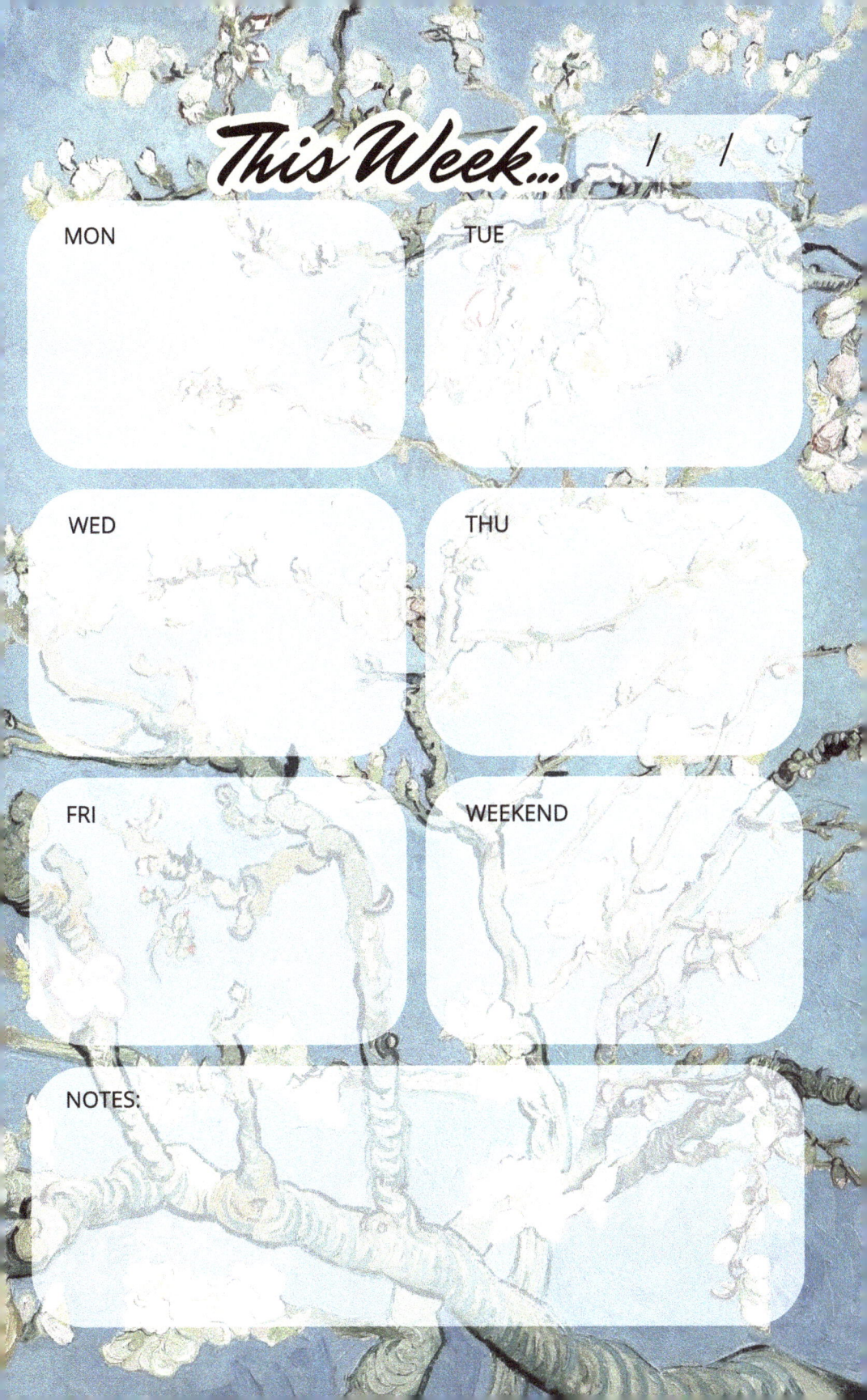

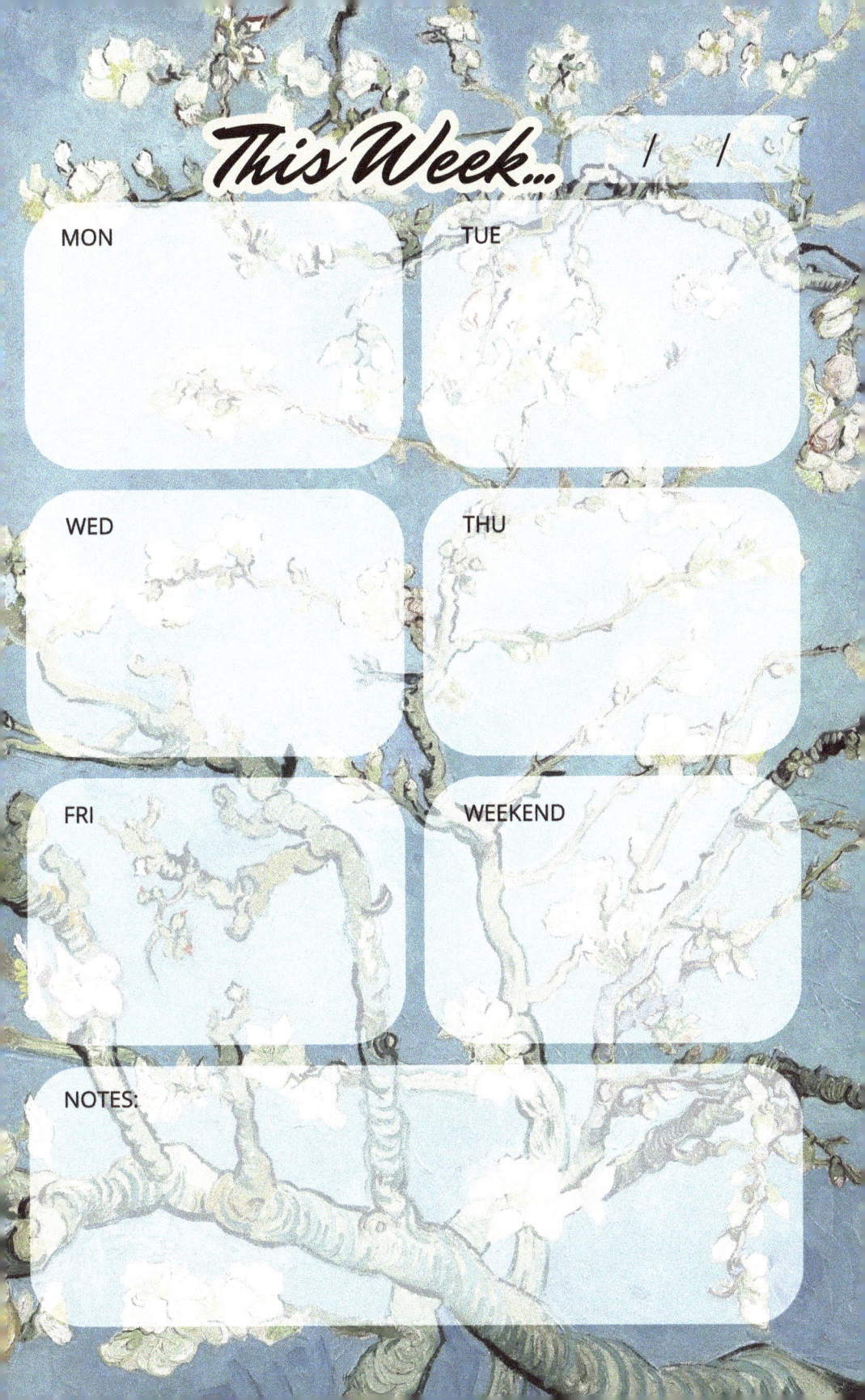

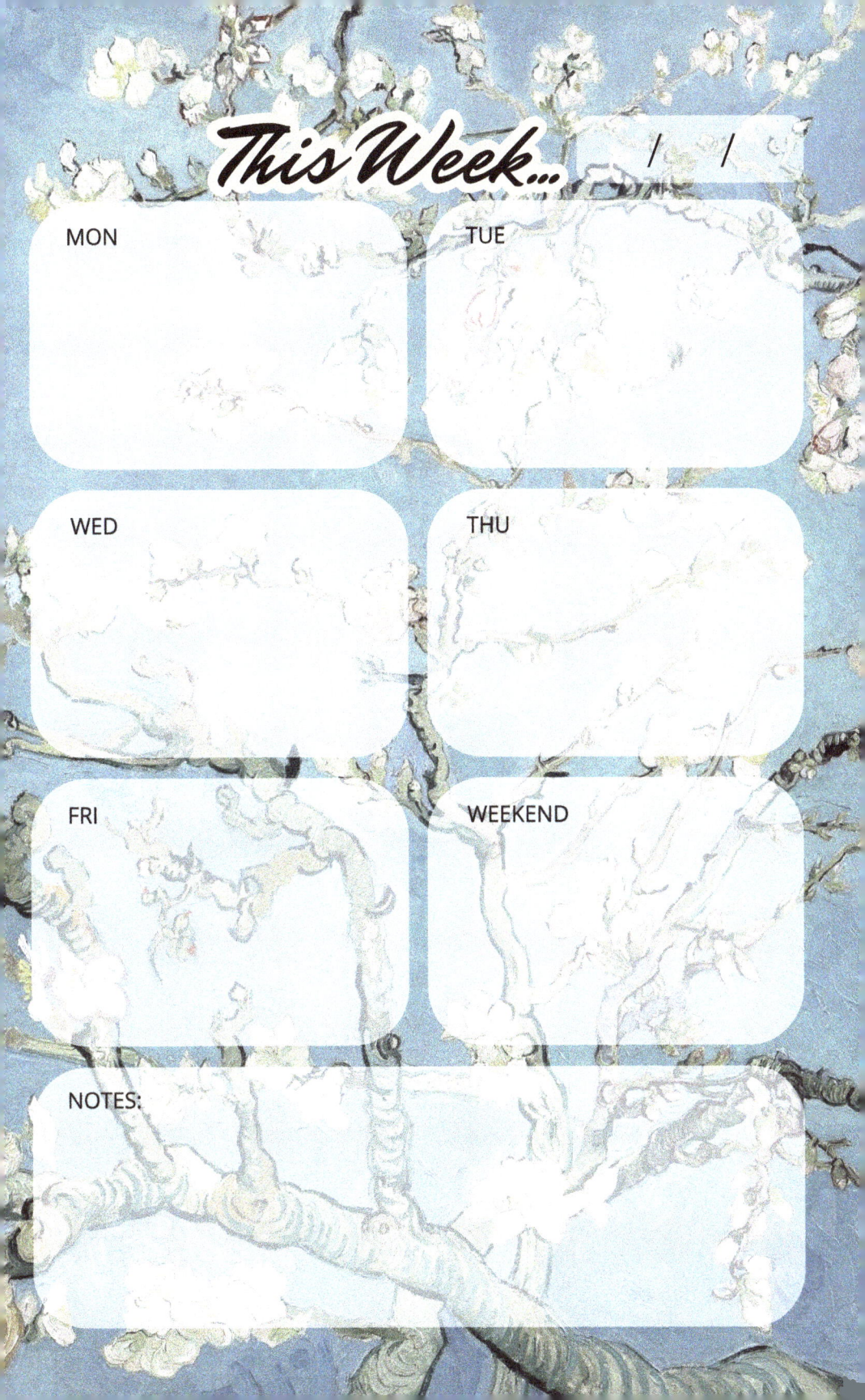

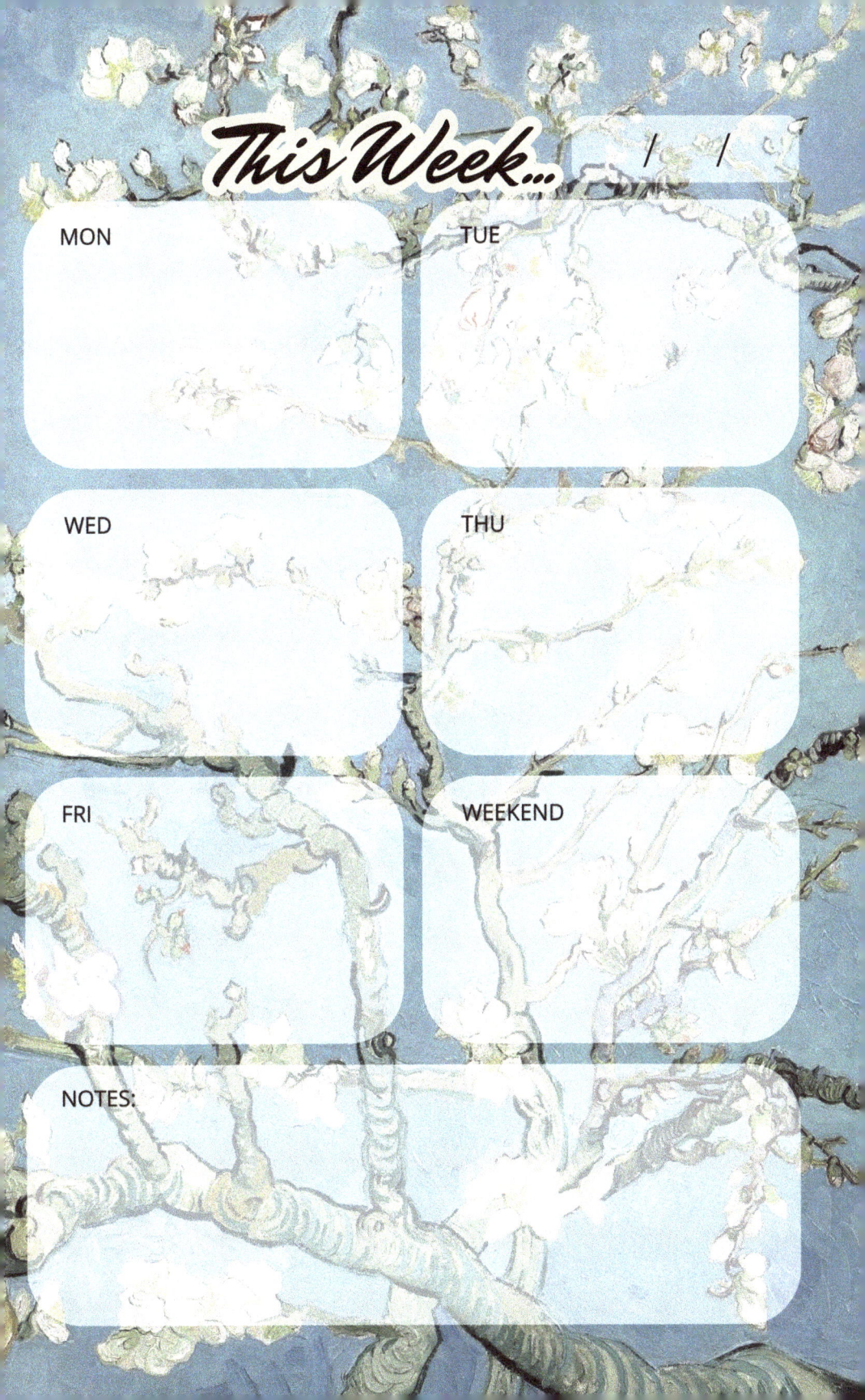

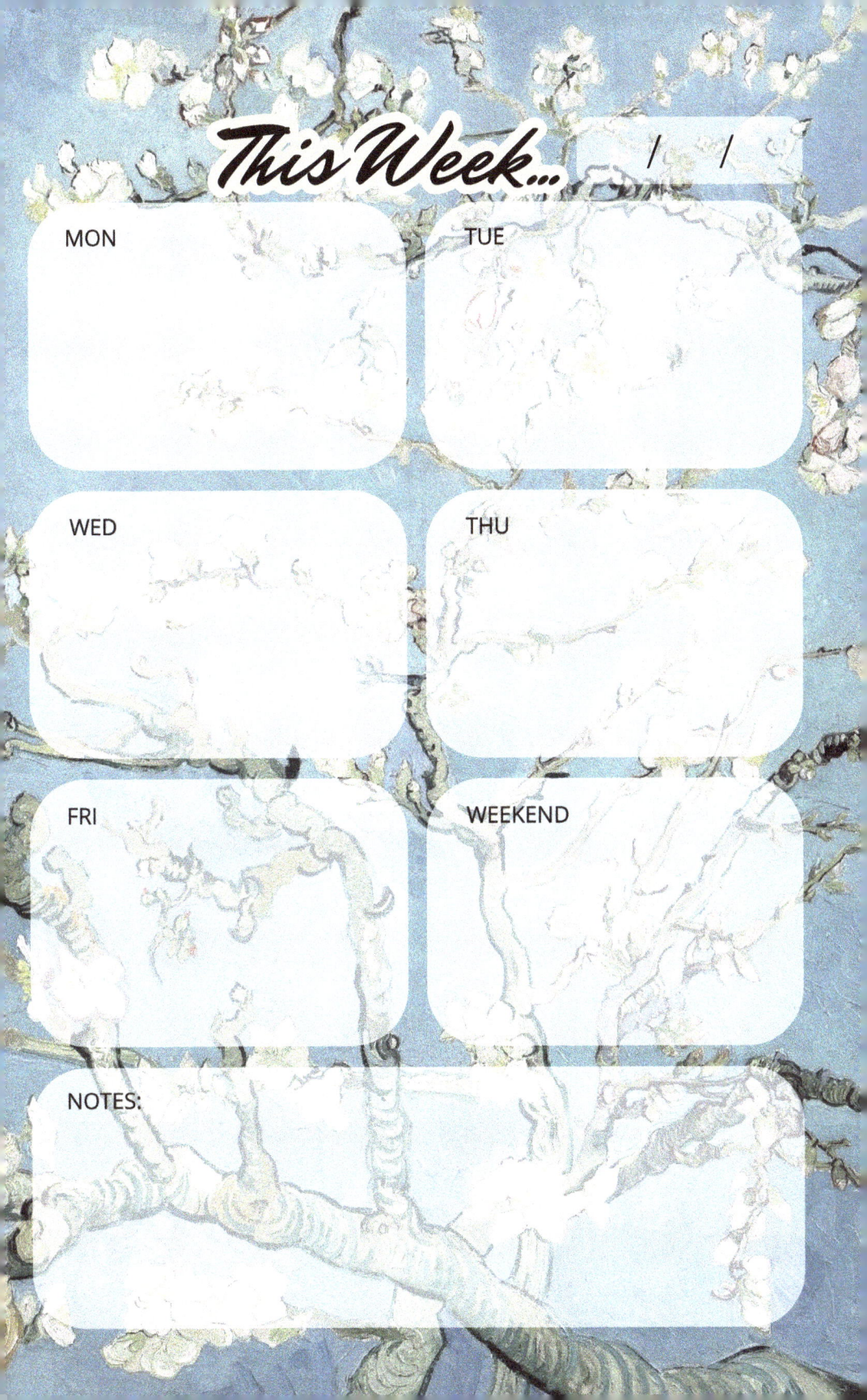

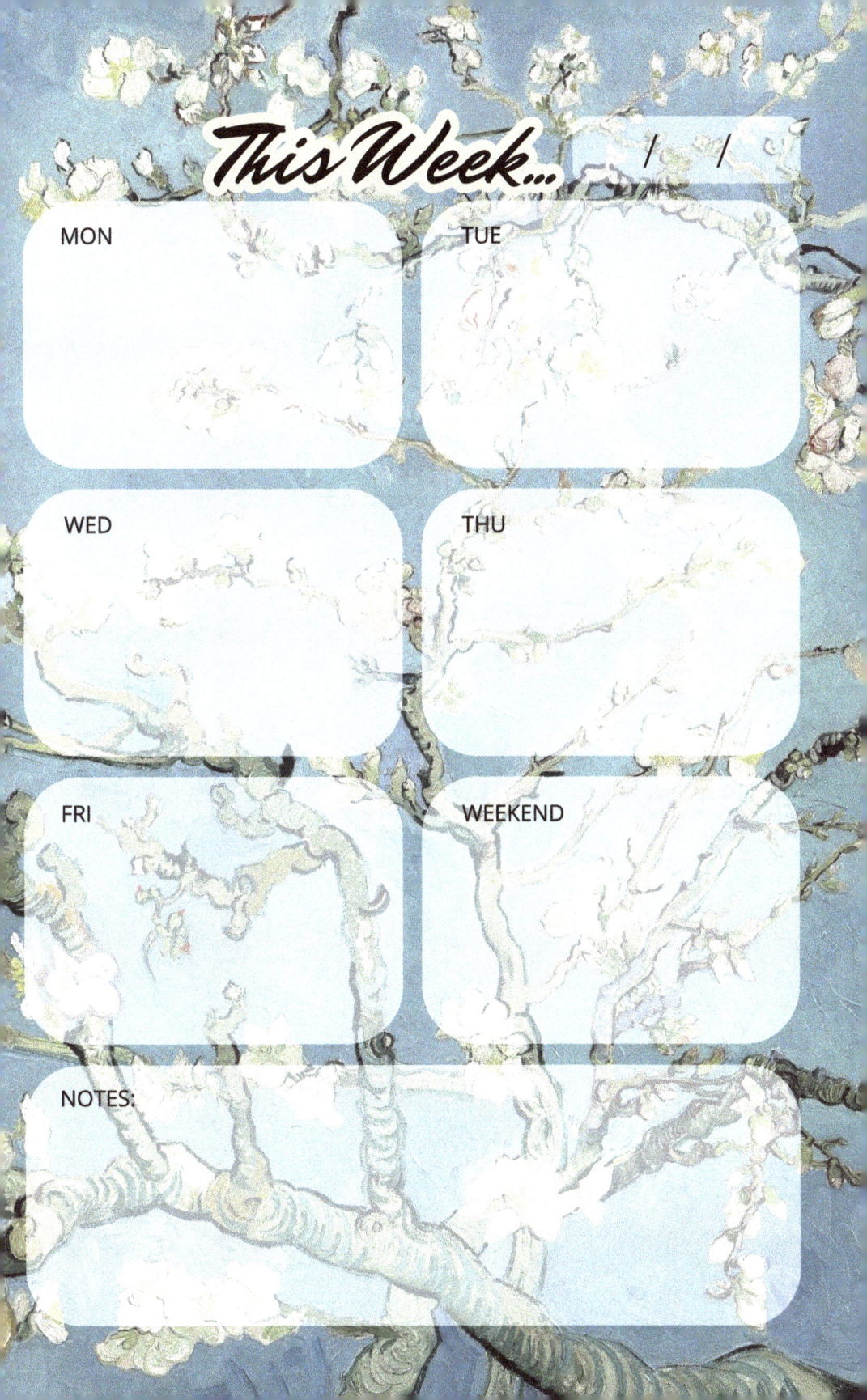

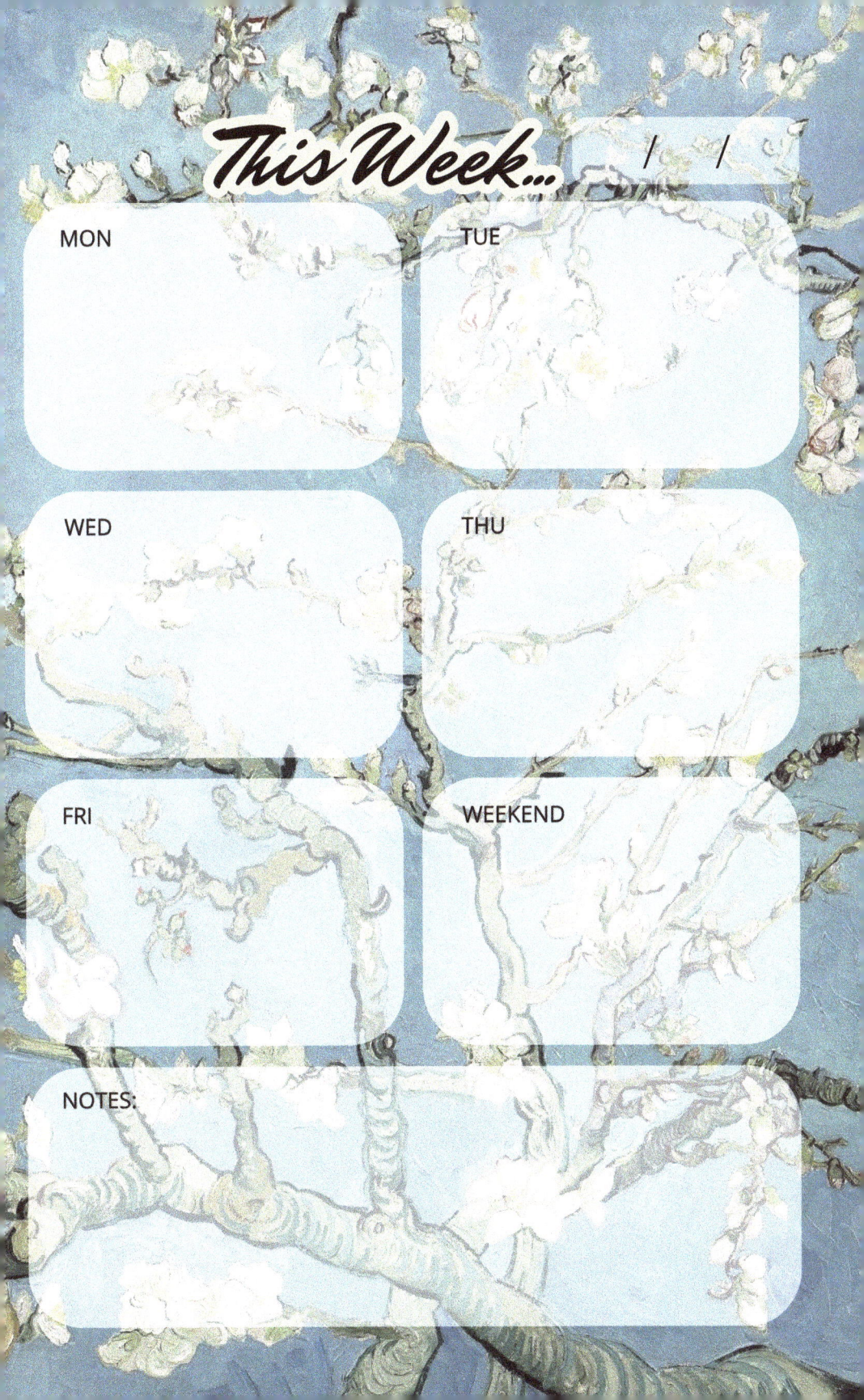

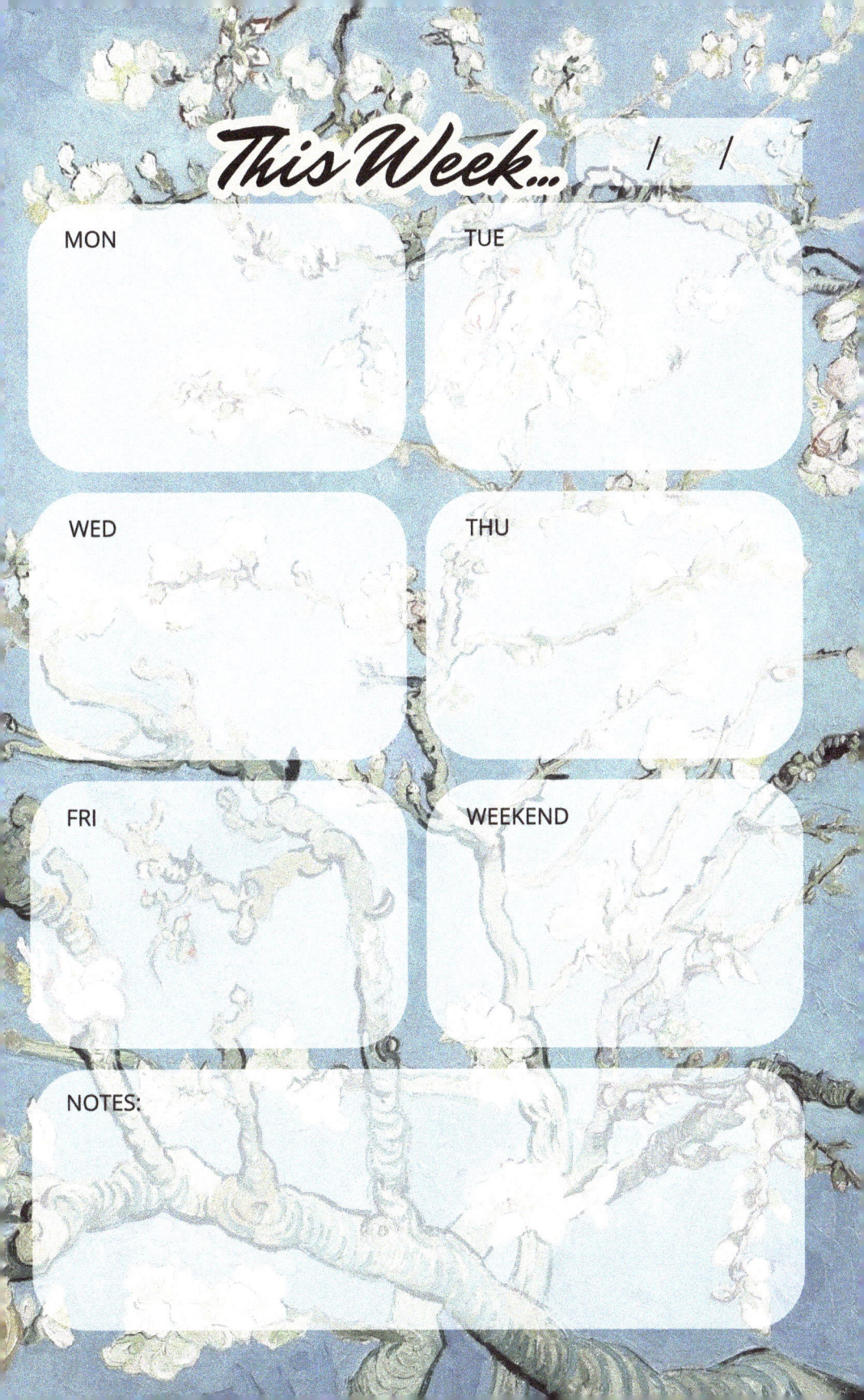

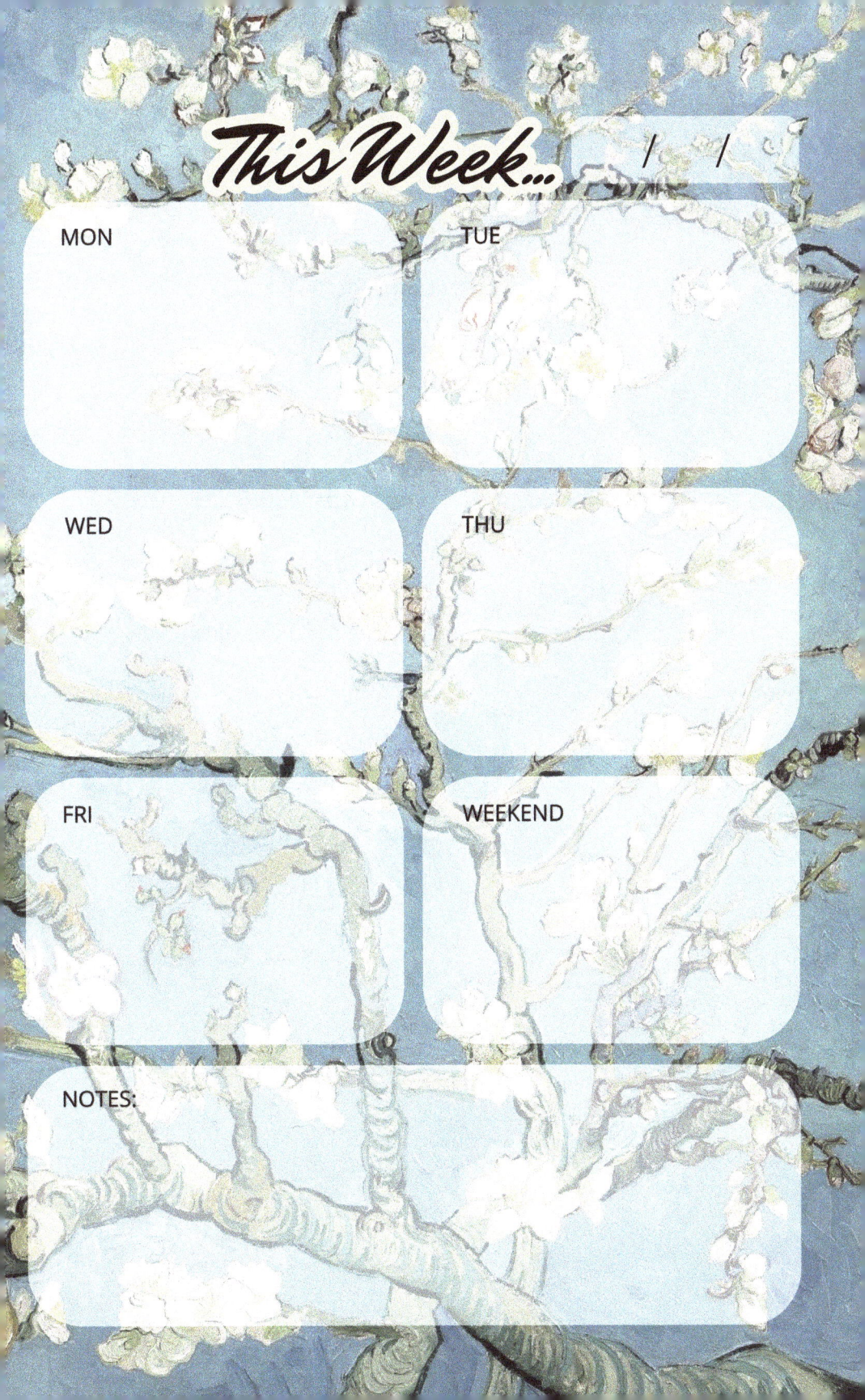

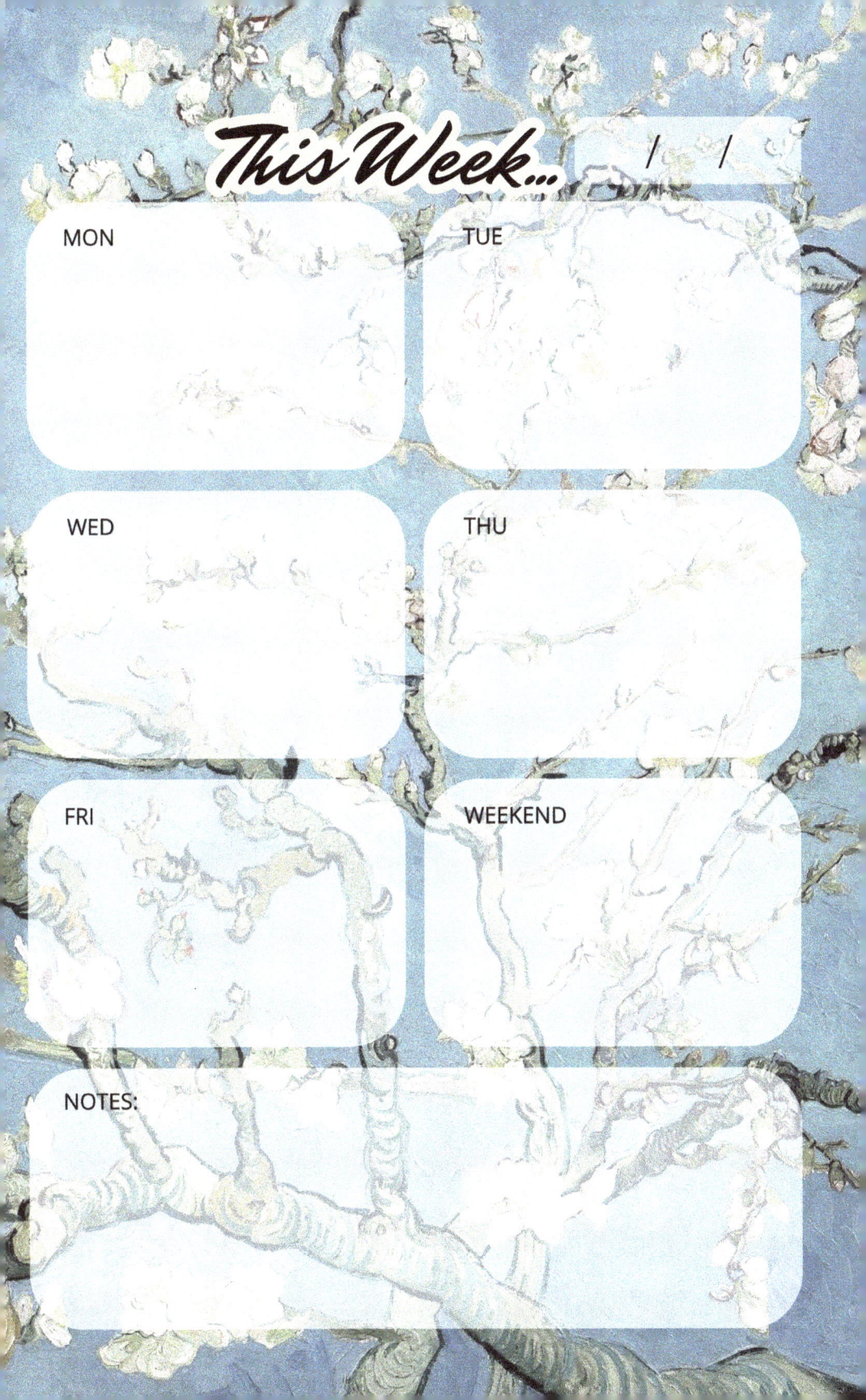

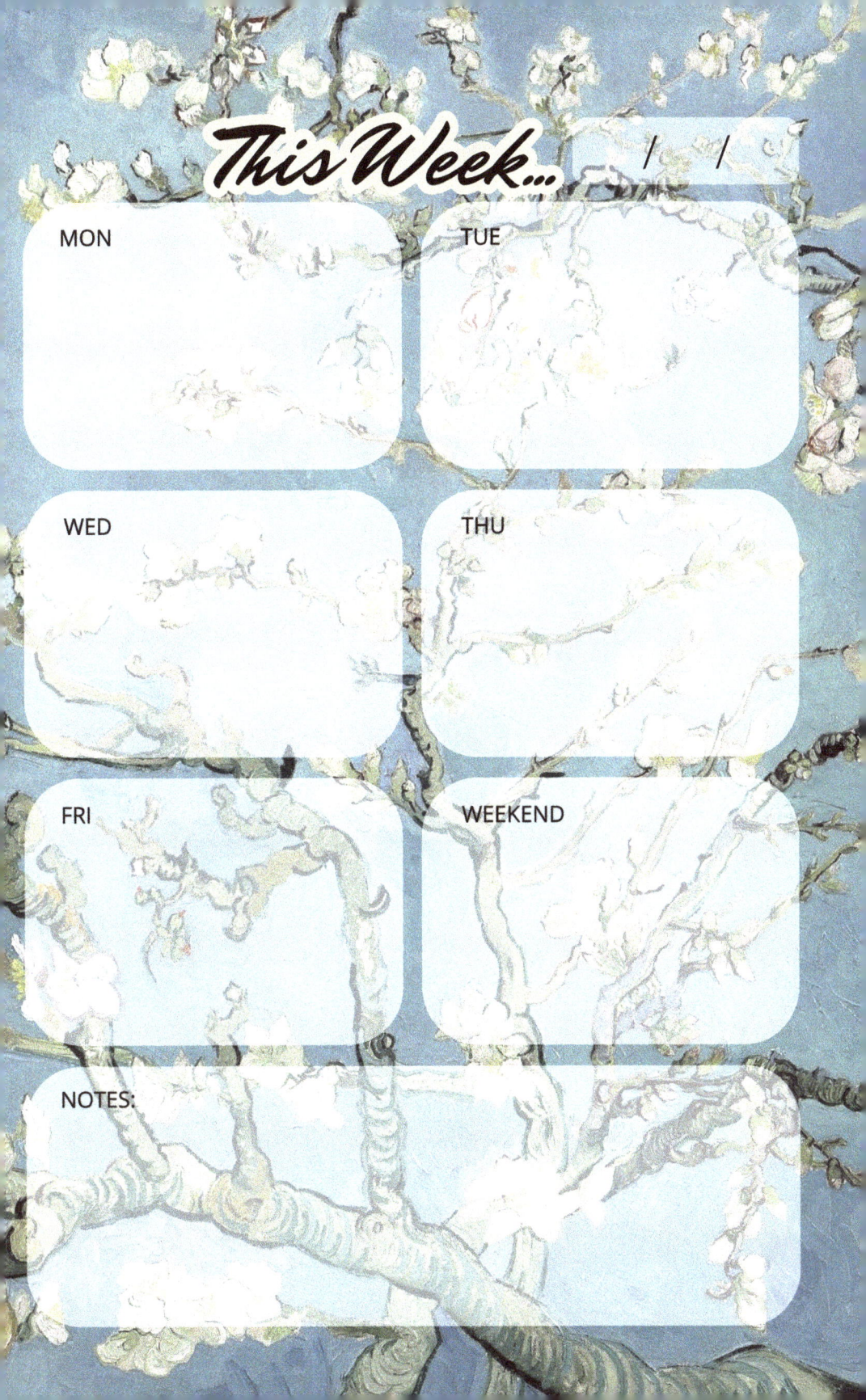

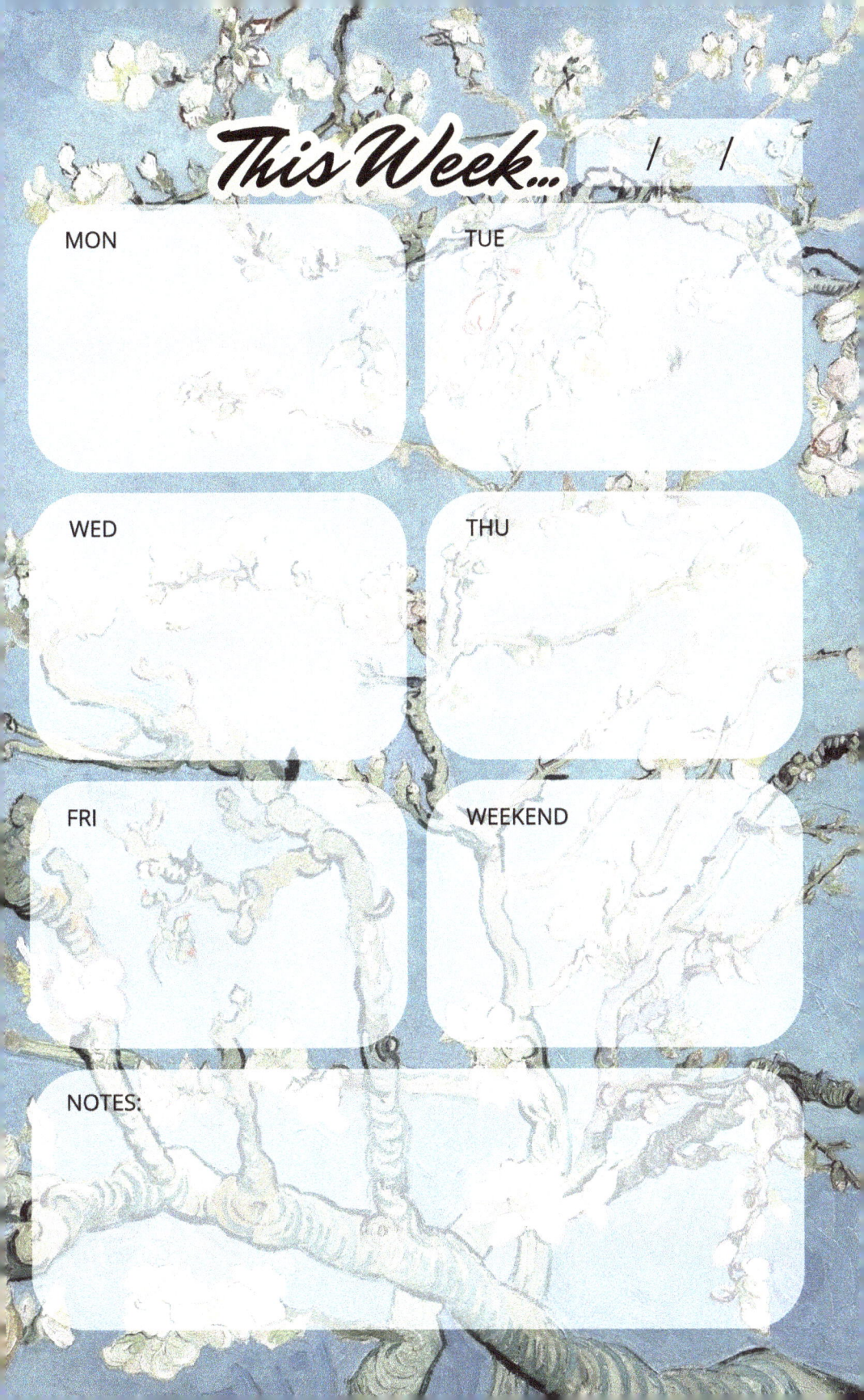

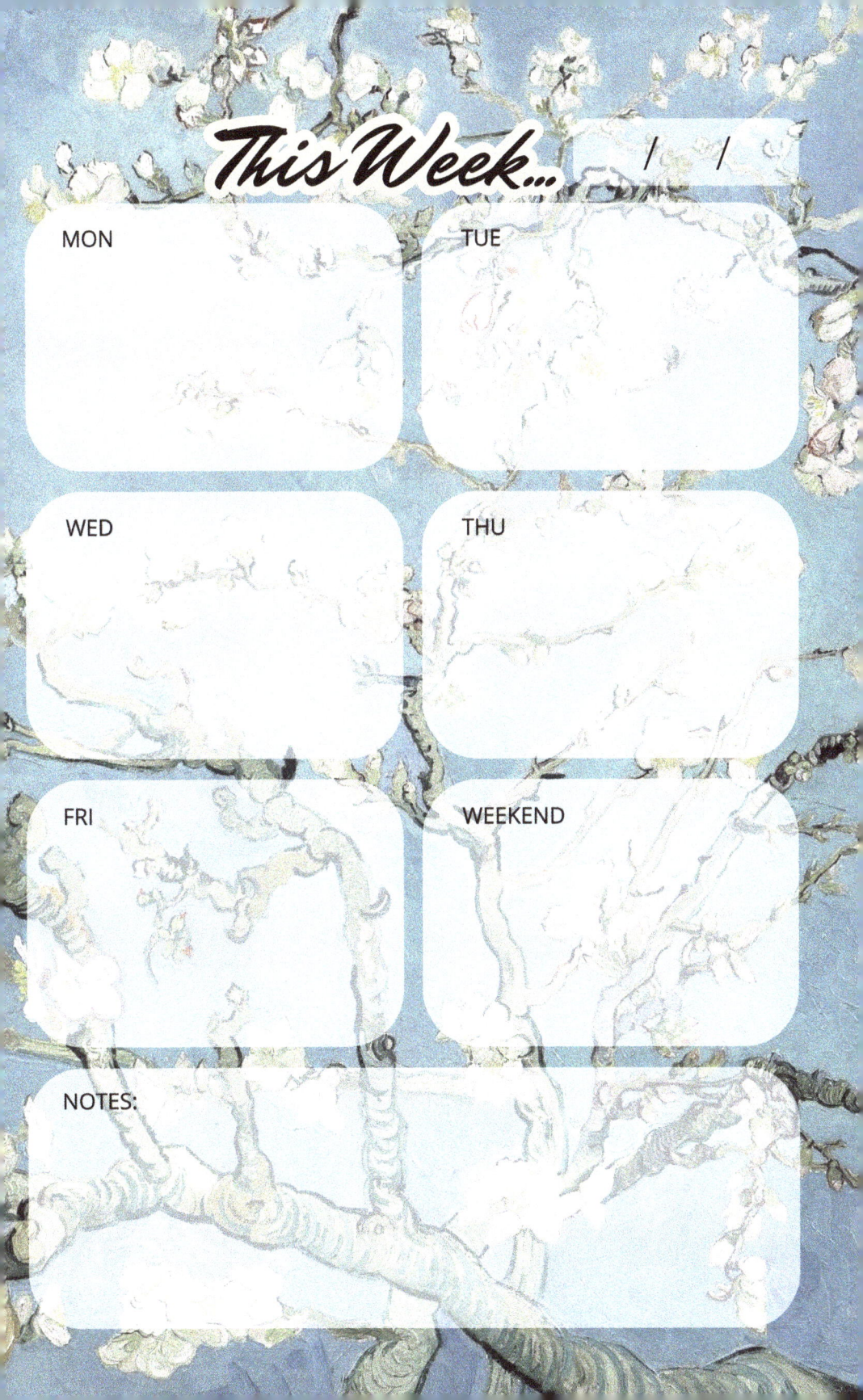

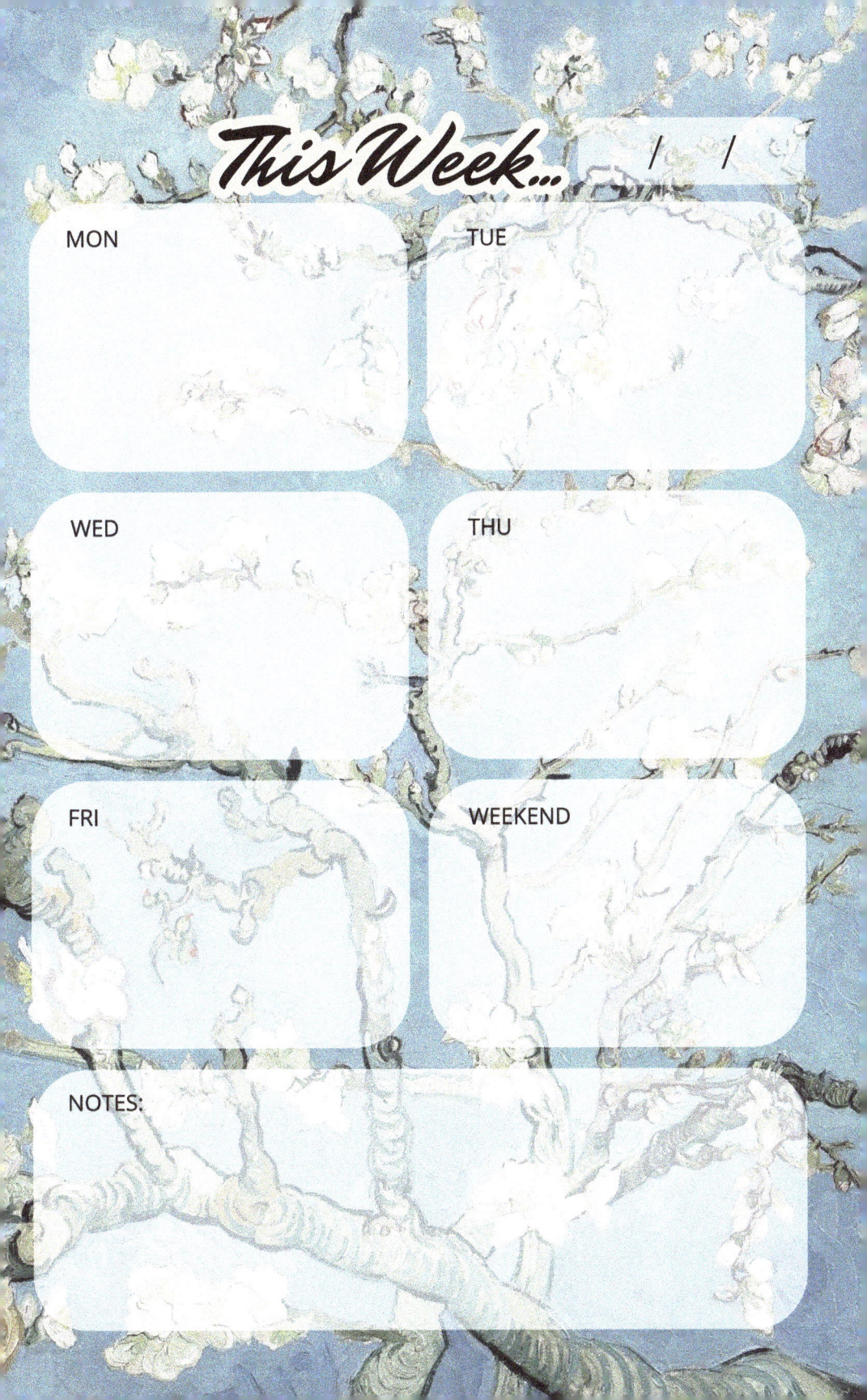

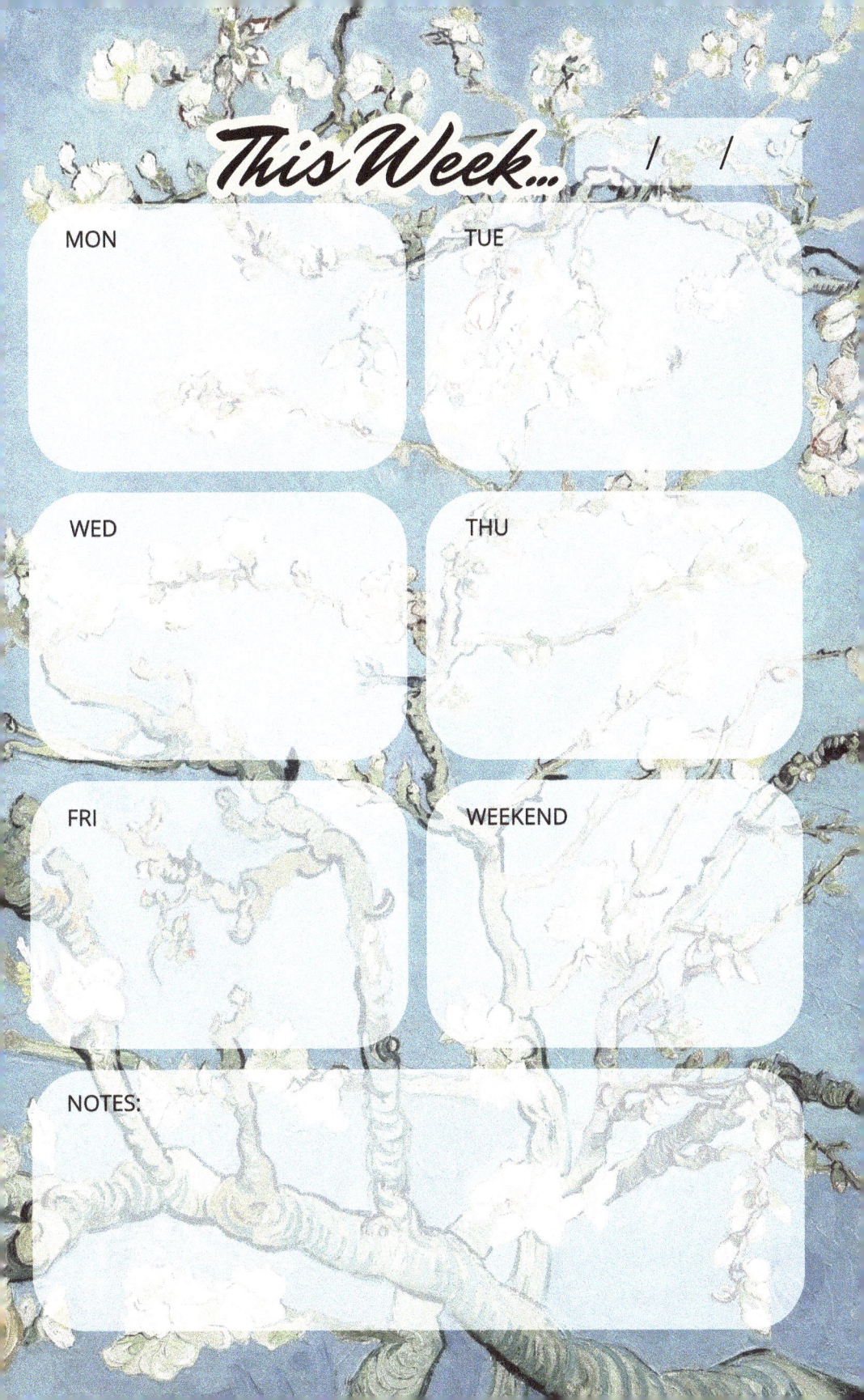

This Week... / /

MON

TUE

WED

THU

FRI

WEEKEND

NOTES:

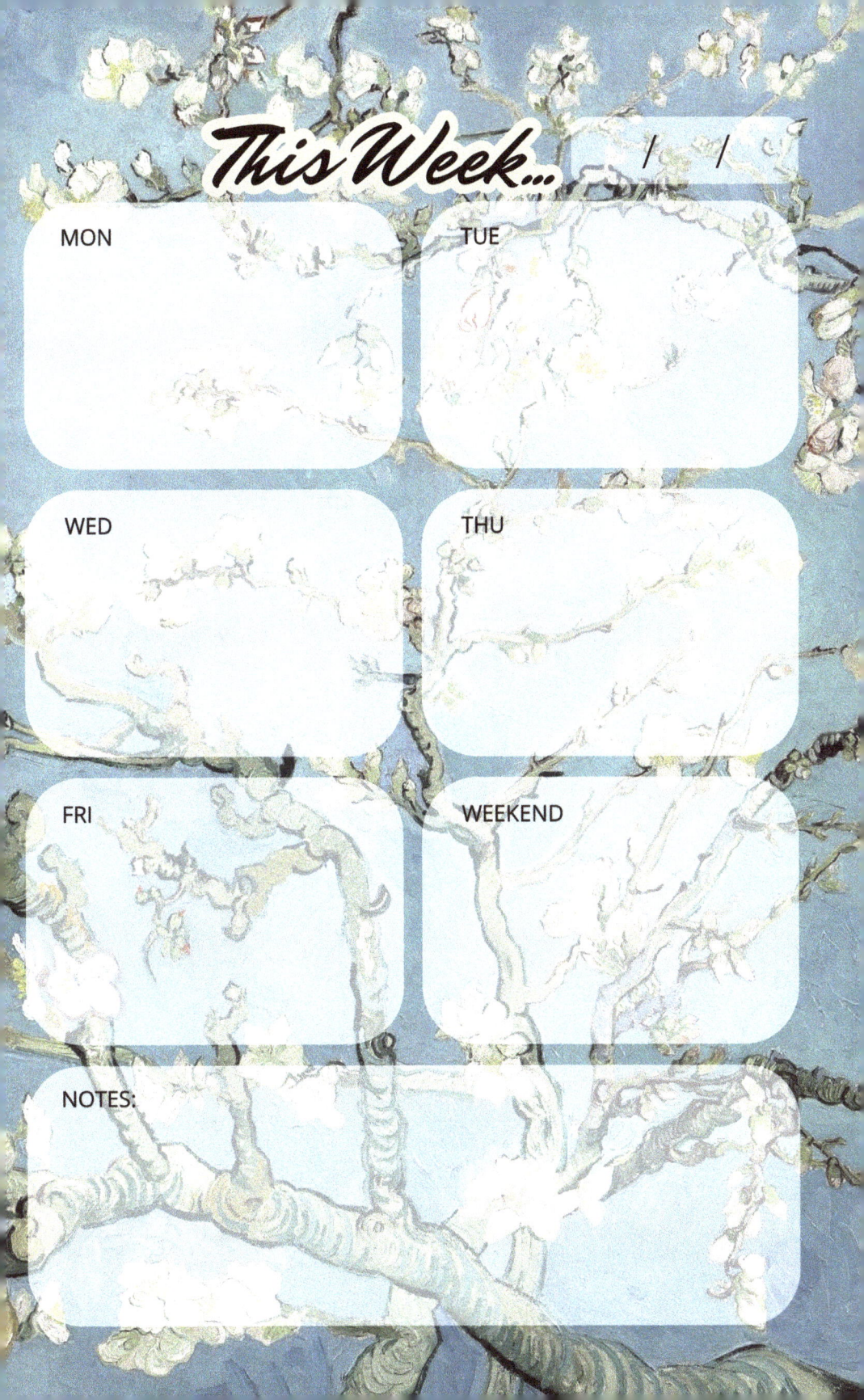

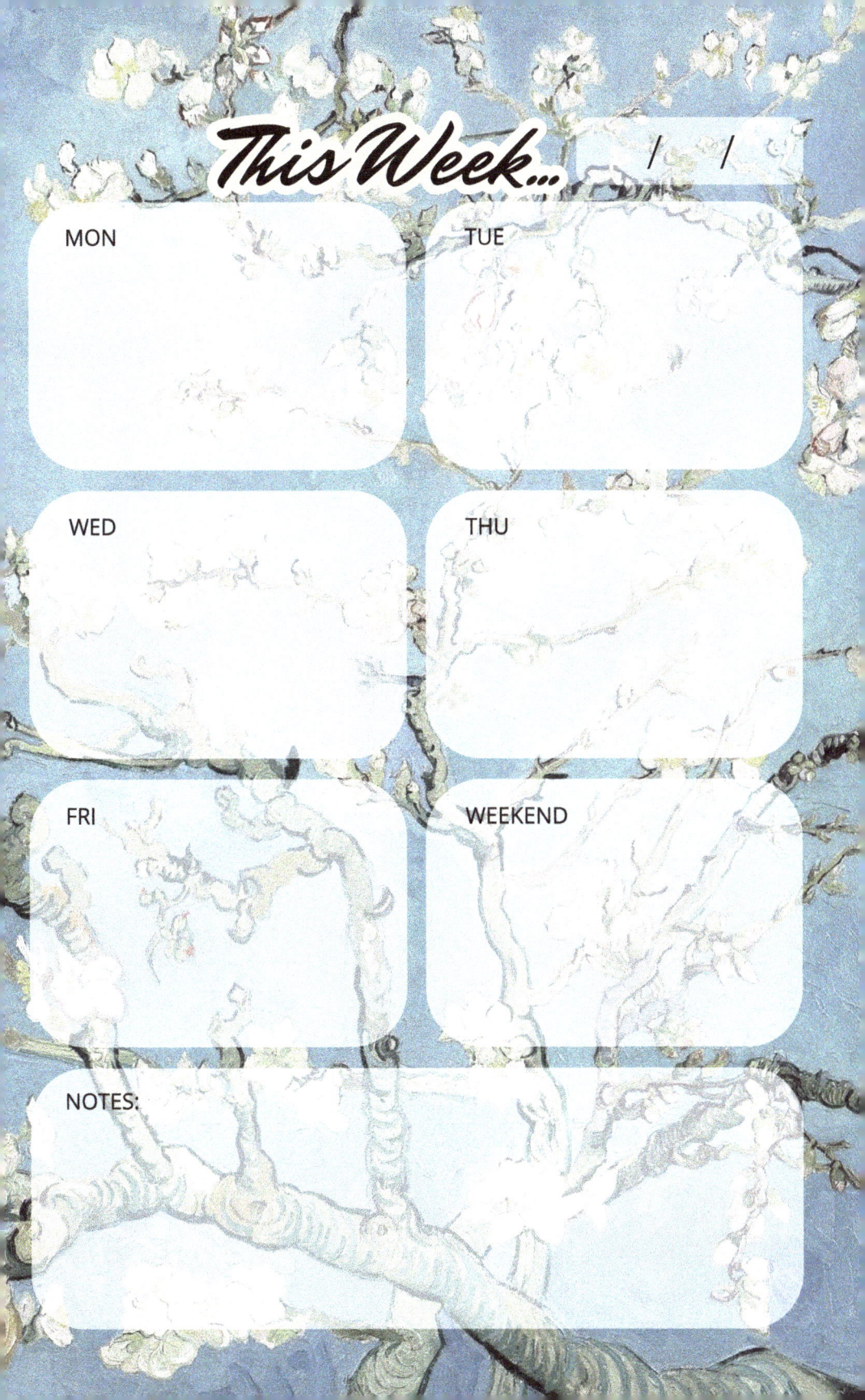

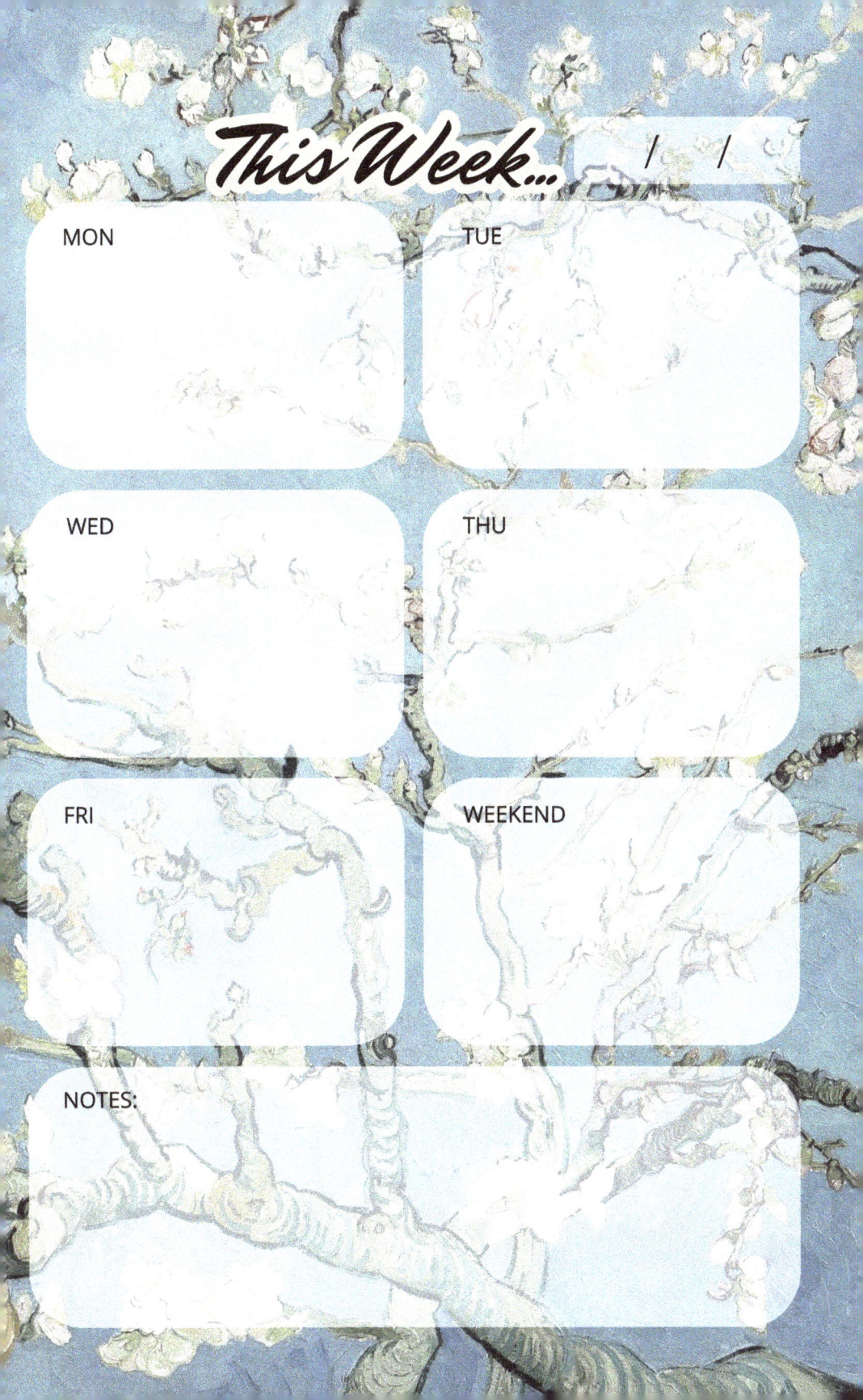

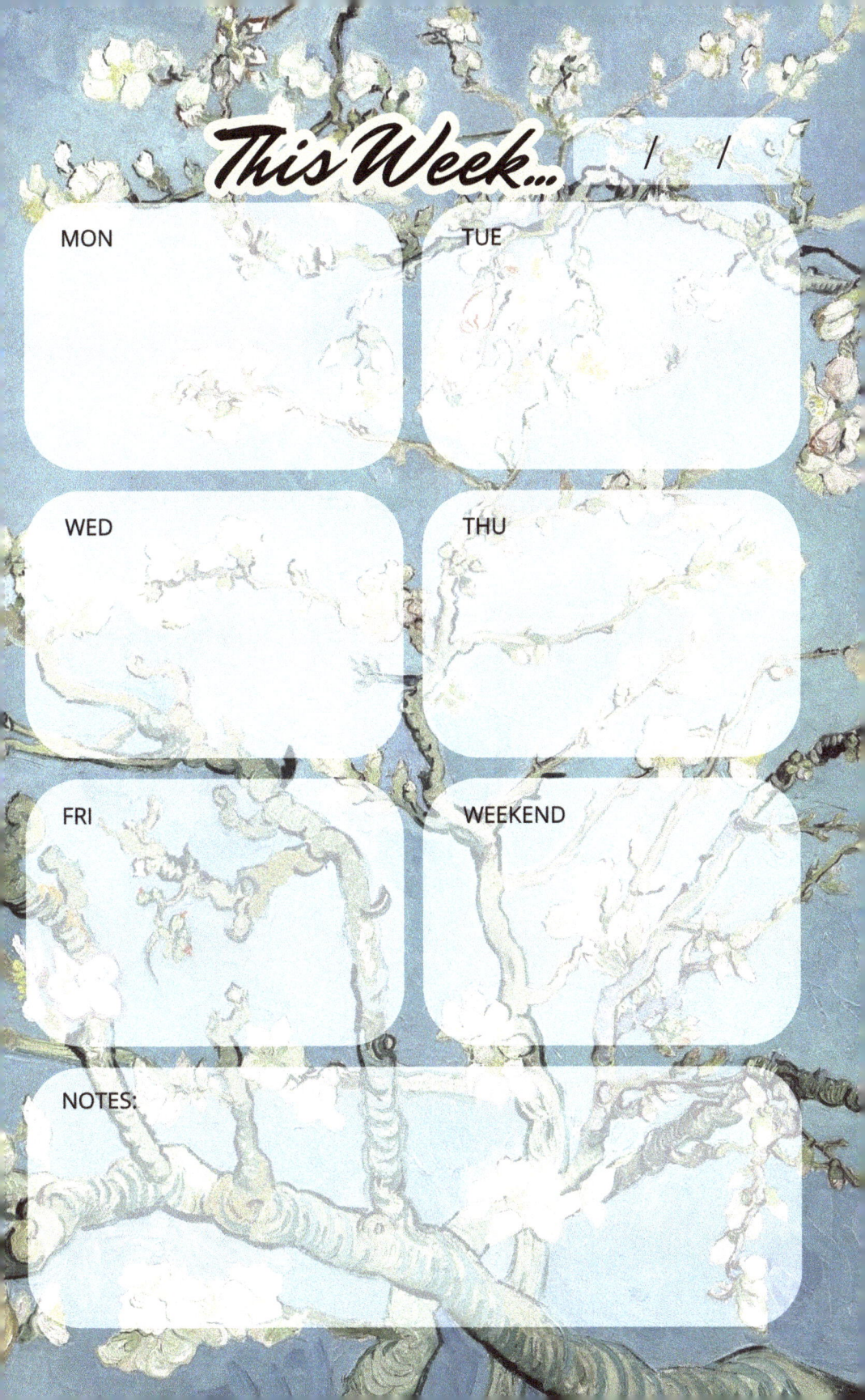

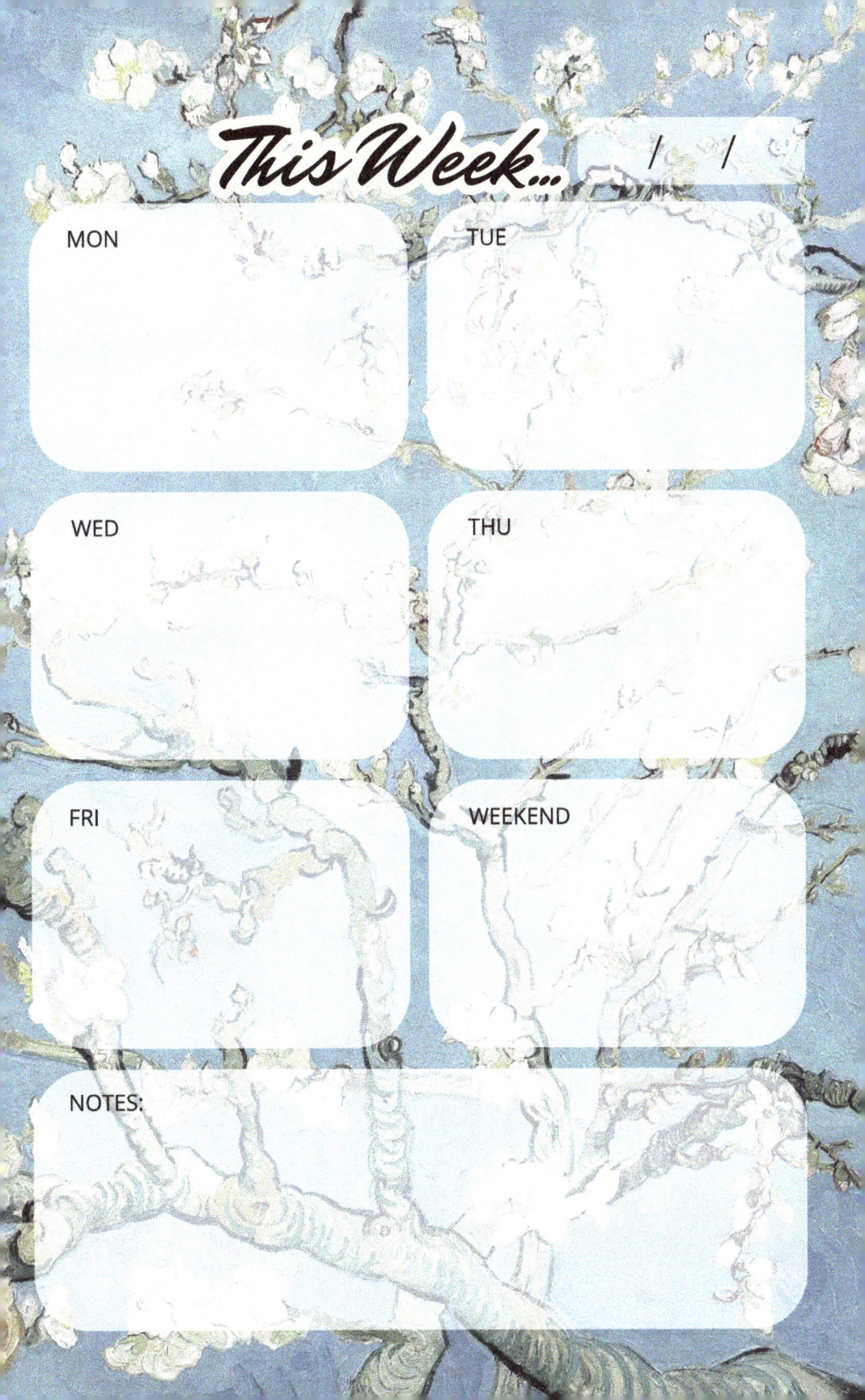

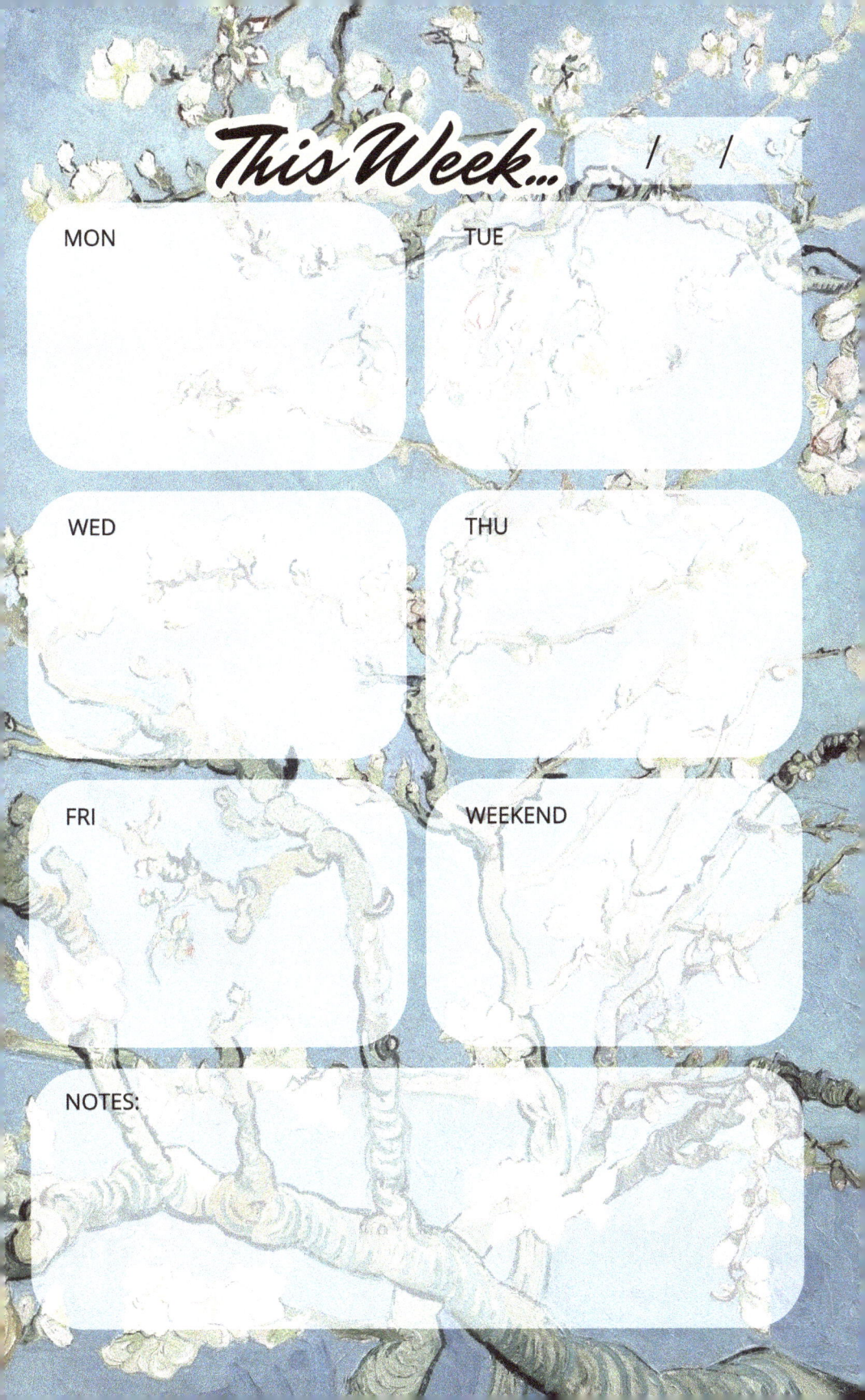

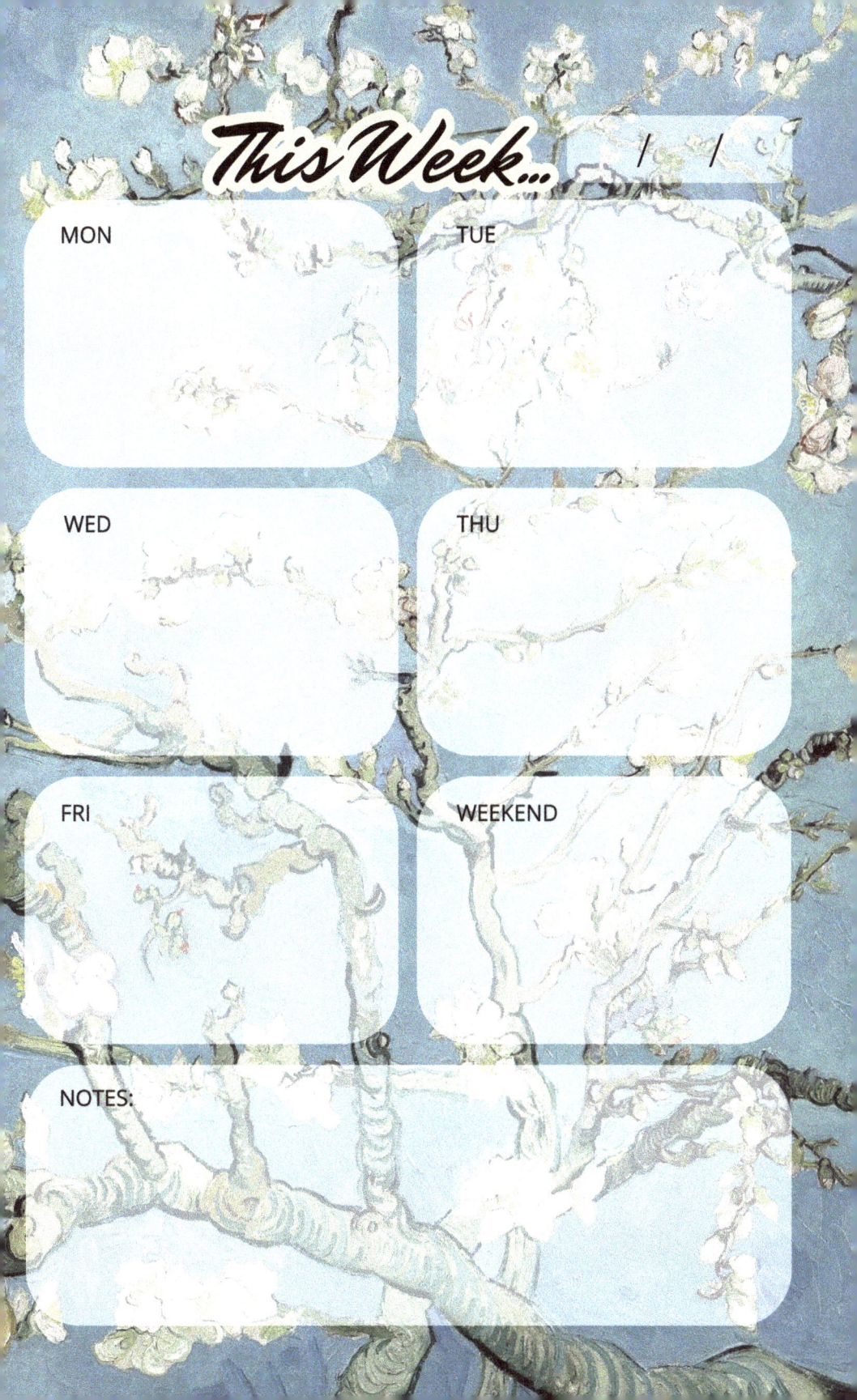

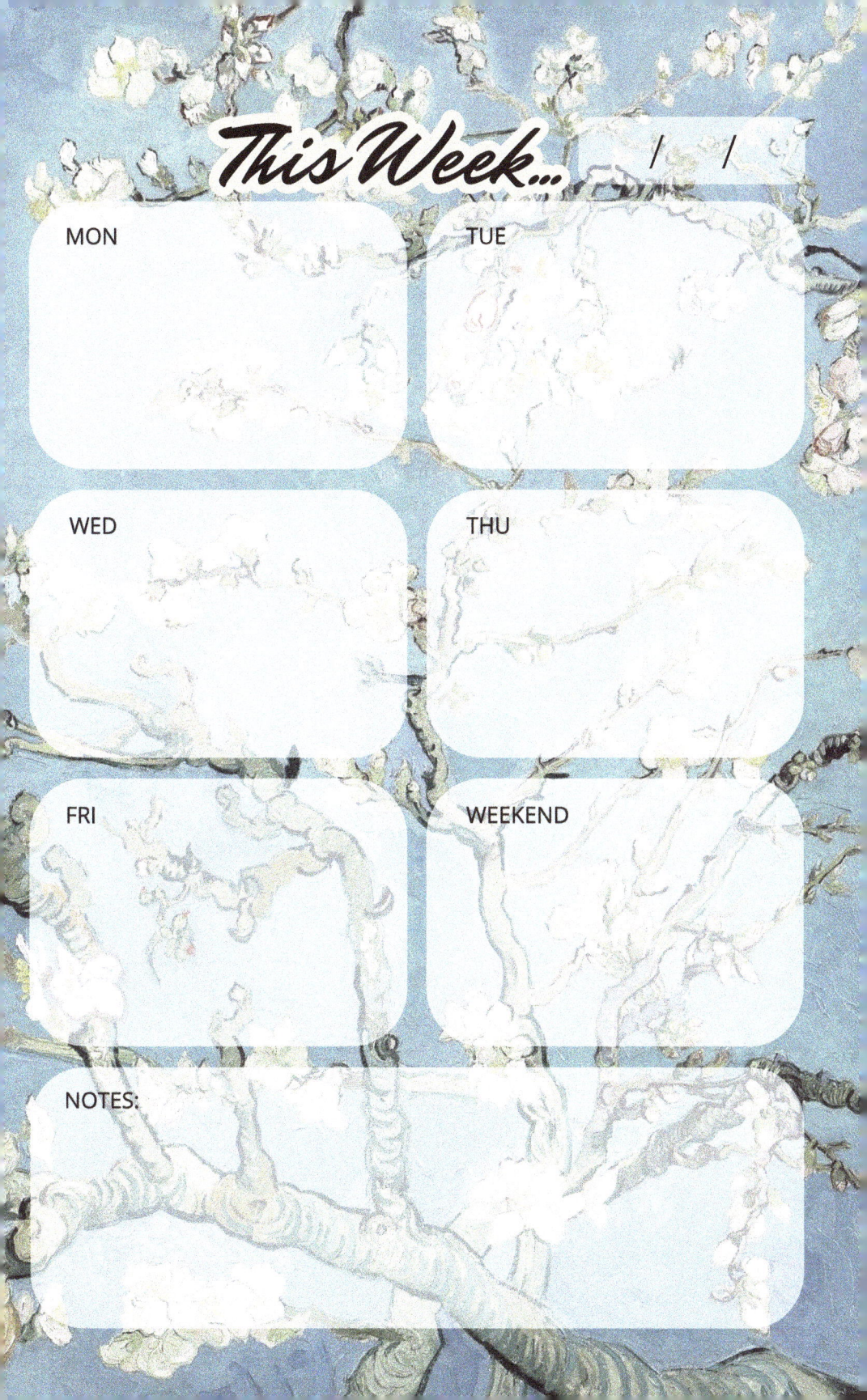

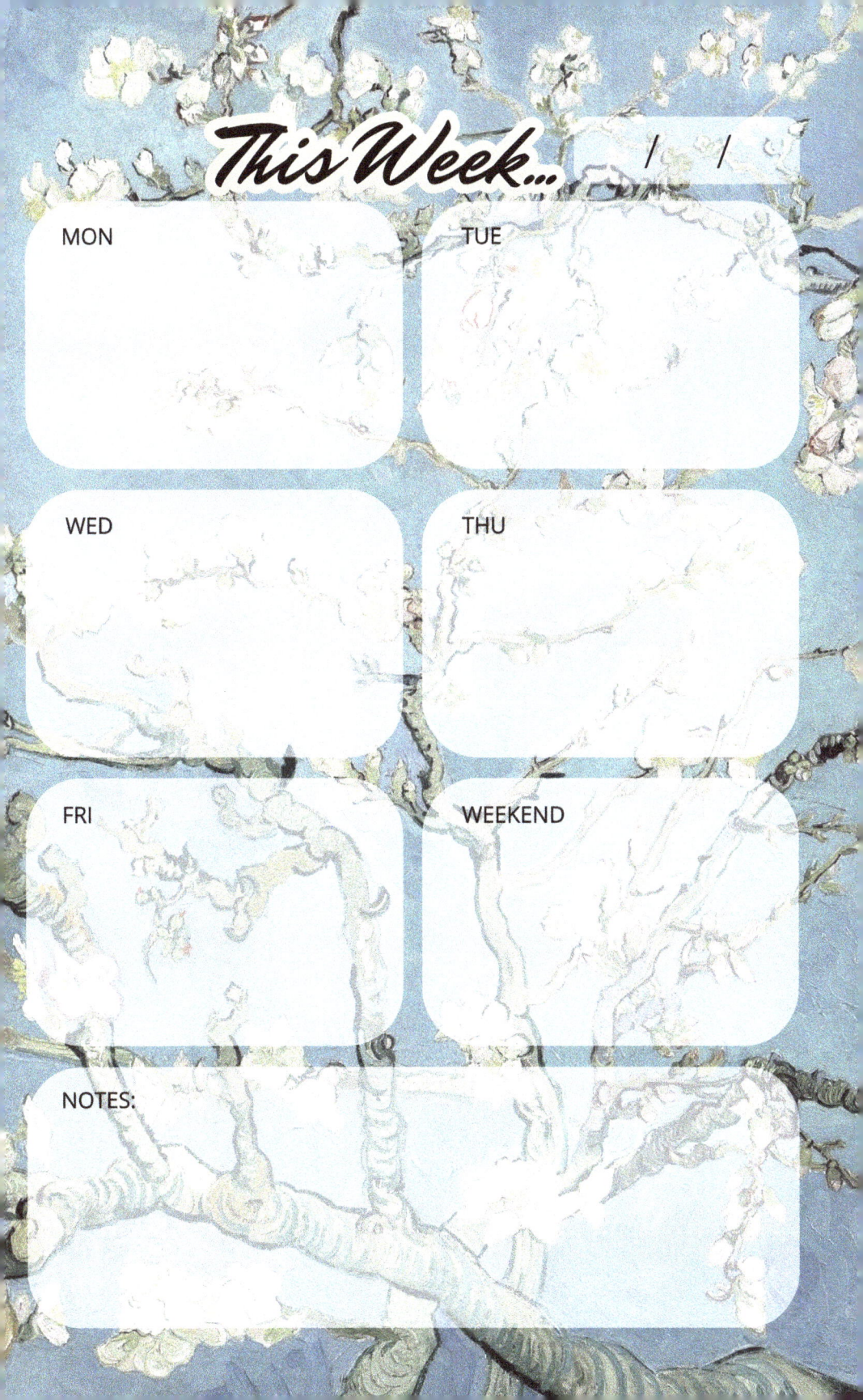

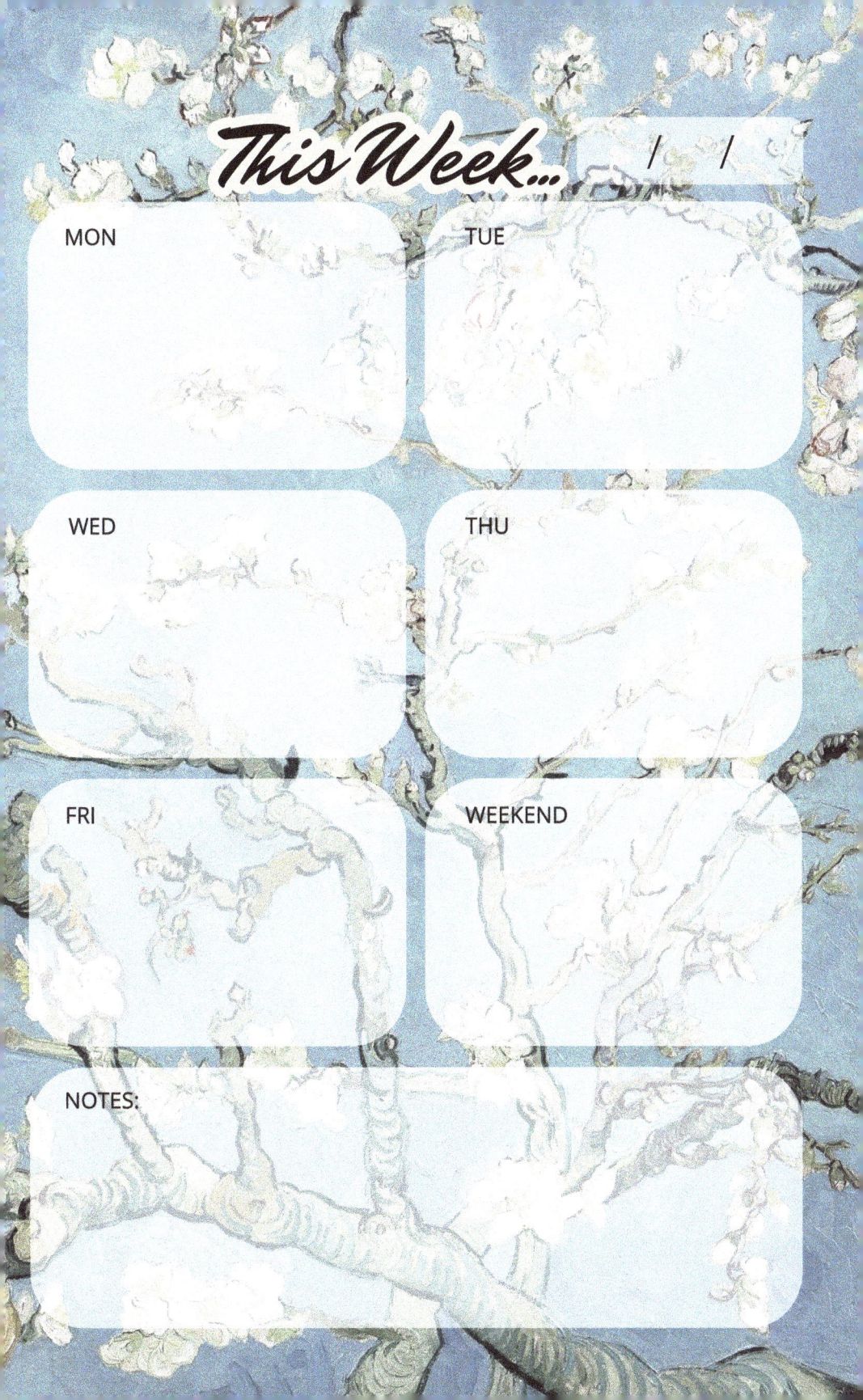

www.ingramcontent.com/pod-product-compliance
Lightning Source LLC
Chambersburg PA
CBHW042129100526
44587CB00026B/4224